DAS MUSEUM NEU ERFINDEN?

Christina Strunck und
Manuel Teget-Welz (Hrsg.)

DAS MUSEUM NEU ERFINDEN?

Dauerausstellungen im Wandel

MICHAEL IMHOF VERLAG

Schriftenreihe des Erlanger Instituts für Kunstgeschichte
herausgegeben von Hans Dickel, Karl Möseneder, Heidrun Stein-Kecks
und Christina Strunck

Band 5

Michael Imhof Verlag GmbH & Co. KG
Stettiner Straße 25 | D-36100 Petersberg
Tel.: 0661/2919166-0 | Fax: 0661/2919166-9
www.imhof-verlag.com | info@imhof-verlag.de

REPRODUKTION UND GESTALTUNG: Patricia Koch, Michael Imhof Verlag
DRUCK: Gutenberg Beuys Feindruckerei GmbH, Langenhagen

Printed in EU

ISBN 978-3-7319-0801-2

INHALT

Christina Strunck | Manuel Teget-Welz

AUSSTELLUNGSKONZEPTE GESTERN – HEUTE – MORGEN

Die internationale Museumslandschaft befindet sich gegenwärtig in einer Phase tiefgreifender Transformationen. Das Wegbrechen des traditionellen „bildungsbürgerlichen" Publikums, gewandelte Erwartungshaltungen der Museumsbesucher, innovative transnationale bzw. globale Perspektiven der kunsthistorischen Forschung, neue Erkenntnisinteressen sowie neuartige technologische Möglichkeiten der Kunstvermittlung stellen zentrale Herausforderungen dar, die die Museumskuratoren von morgen intensiv reflektieren müssen, wenn die Institution Museum zukunftsfähig bleiben will.

Das Sammeln und Ausstellen von Kunst hat bereits eine jahrhundertelange Geschichte. Die frühneuzeitlichen Kunst- und Wunderkammern präsentierten Kunstwerke neben natur- und völkerkundlichen Objekten, um den Makrokosmos im Mikrokosmos abzubilden. Hiervon grenzte sich das Konzept der Galerie im Barockzeitalter ab, da sie oft dem panegyrischen Herrscherlob als Teil einer übergreifenden Gesamtaussage diente. Um 1800 konzentrierten sich die jetzt in ganz Europa gegründeten öffentlichen Kunstmuseen zunehmend auf Werke der klassischen Gattungen Malerei und Skulptur, die streng nach Schulen und Epochen geordnet wurden. Die Idee des sogenannten *period room* folgte in der zweiten Hälfte des 19. Jahrhunderts; hier wurden Objekte der unterschiedlichsten Gattungen wieder zusammen in einem Ambiente ausgestellt, das man historischen Räumlichkeiten nachempfand. Den konzeptionellen Gegenentwurf lieferte im 20. Jahrhundert der *white cube*, in dem durch möglichst neutrale Gestaltung der Ausstellungsarchitektur das Kunstwerk vor allem als ästhetisches Objekt zur Wirkung gebracht werden sollte.

Heute sind Kunstmuseen ein weltweites Massenphänomen. Für ihre Konzeption werden traditionell erprobte Ausstellungsformate – wie die Dauerausstellung mit Werken einer Gattung – hinterfragt und mit Neuansätzen in Konkurrenz gestellt, die auf ältere universale Präsentationskonzepte zurückgeführt werden können. Aufgrund der gesteigerten Relevanz der Kulturgeschichte bleibt die Exponatauswahl dabei nicht auf Werke der klassischen Gattungen der bildenden Kunst beschränkt, sondern bindet vielmehr Gegenstände der materiellen Kultur – etwa Forschungsinstrumente oder Kleidungs- und Schmuckstücke – ein. Die Objekte sollen dabei dem

Betrachter in ihrem historischen wie geistesgeschichtlichen Kontext begreifbar gemacht werden. Neben den Forschungsergebnissen aus der Kunst- und Kulturgeschichte gewinnen aber auch Kunsttechnologie, Kunstpädagogik und Betriebswirtschaftslehre (insbesondere Marketing) zunehmend stärkere Bedeutung bei der Planung und Durchführung von Ausstellungen.

Wie dieser knappe Blick in Vergangenheit und Gegenwart des Museumswesens deutlich macht, sind die Ausstellungskonzepte, Organisationssysteme und Präsentationsformen von Kunstwerken und Kulturgütern seit ihren frühneuzeitlichen Anfängen bis heute unterschiedlichsten, zum Teil konträren Umbildungsprozessen unterworfen. Entsprechend sind für die Zukunft weitere gravierende Veränderungen zu erwarten, nicht zuletzt wegen des stetigen gesellschaftlichen Wandels und des damit sich verändernden Publikums im Museum, dem immer mehr nach dem Konzept des partizipativen Museums unter anderem die Möglichkeit zur Gestaltung eigener Ausstellungsinhalte angeboten wird. Zu den zukünftigen Herausforderungen gehören aber auch die neuen Möglichkeiten im Einsatz digitaler Medien, sei es beispielsweise bei der Präsentation digitaler Kunst im virtuellen Ausstellungskonzept oder beim Einsatz digitaler Kommunikationsgeräte als Instrument der Kunstvermittlung.

Um diesen Herausforderungen zu begegnen, haben wir am Institut für Kunstgeschichte der Friedrich-Alexander-Universität Erlangen-Nürnberg zusätzlich zum bereits etablierten Masterschwerpunkt „Museumsstudien" neue museologische Lehrformate entwickelt. 2016 und 2017 fanden zwei international ausgeschriebene museologische Studienkurse statt; seit 2018 läuft das von der VolkswagenStiftung finanzierte Forschungskolleg „Modellierung von Kulturgeschichte am Beispiel des Germanischen Nationalmuseums: Vermittlungskonzepte für das 21. Jahrhundert", in dem sechs Doktorand/inn/en parallel zur Arbeit an einem kulturgeschichtlichen Dissertationsthema an Beständen des Germanischen Nationalmuseums in Nürnberg neue Vermittlungsformen entwickeln und erproben können.

Die beiden erwähnten Studienkurse nahmen zwei komplementär aufeinander bezogene Phänomene in den Blick: 2016 ging es zunächst um Dauerausstellungen, 2017 dann um Sonder- bzw. Jubiläumsausstellungen. Das Jahr 2017 war für die Reflexion der letztgenannten Thematik optimal geeignet, wurde doch das 500. Reformationsjubiläum allerorten gefeiert. So ergab sich die seltene Chance, mehrere Sonderausstellungen zum selben Anlass vergleichend zu analysieren. Die vom DAAD und der Dr. German Schweiger-Stiftung geförderte knapp zweiwöchige Veranstaltung ermöglichte es Teilnehmer/innen aus dem In- und Ausland, fünf große Reformations-Jubiläumsausstellungen in Berlin, Coburg, Nürnberg, Wittenberg und auf der Wartburg zu besichtigen, ihre jeweiligen Stärken und Schwächen herauszuarbeiten sowie die konzeptionellen Voraussetzungen und praktischen Herausforderungen im Gespräch mit den Kurator/inn/en und wissenschaftlichen Beiräten zu diskutieren.

Der vorliegende Band geht auf den Studienkurs 2016 zurück, der es sich zum Ziel gemacht hatte, durch die Auseinandersetzung mit historischen und aktuellen Ausstellungsformen sowie im Dialog mit international renommierten Experten Ideen für das Museum der Zukunft zu entwickeln. Seinem Titel „Ausstellungskonzepte gestern – heute – morgen" entsprechend, besaß der Kurs eine dreiteilige Struktur. In der Sektion „Ausstellungskonzepte – gestern" wurden in Referaten wichtige historische Präsentationsformen auf Basis neuester Forschung vorgestellt und aus verschiedenen Perspektiven an konkreten Beispielen analysiert. Jeder Tag stand dabei unter einem übergeordneten Thema: Kunst- und Wunderkammer, Galerie, Die Anfänge des öffentlichen Museums und Museumskonzepte der Moderne. Der Block „Ausstellungskonzepte – heute" gab Einblick in aktuelle Projekte des Germanischen Nationalmuseums und der Museen der Stadt Nürnberg und eröffnete einen auf zentrale Aufgabenfelder fokussierten Dialog mit etablierten Museumskuratoren. Im Rahmen der Ortstermine berichteten sechs führende Mitarbeiter/innen der in Nürnberg angesiedelten Museen praxisnah an tagesaktuellen Beispielen von ihrer Arbeit rund um das Thema Ausstellungskonzepte aus der Perspektive ihrer jeweiligen Position. Das darauf folgende internationale Symposium thematisierte schließlich durch die Vorträge namhafter Expert/ inn/en aus Museum und Universität „Ausstellungskonzepte – morgen" und gab den Kursteilnehmer/inne/n die Möglichkeit, ihre zuvor entwickelten Ideen in der Diskussion mit den Vortragenden weiter zu vertiefen.

Das Symposium widmete sich zukünftigen Ausstellungsformaten sowie den damit verbundenen Umbildungsprozessen und Innovationen im internationalen Museumswesen. In sechs Beiträgen wurden neue Tendenzen, Chancen und Herausforderungen für zukünftige Projekte im internationalen Museumswesen vorgestellt und diskutiert: Welche Konsequenzen hat der Paradigmenwechsel von der klassischen Kunst- zur fächerübergreifenden Kulturgeschichte für das Ausstellungswesen? Wie kann die interinstitutionelle Zusammenarbeit zwischen Museum und Universität bei der Entwicklung innovativer Ausstellungskonzepte aussehen? Wie lässt sich das Konzept des partizipativen Museums in der Praxis umsetzen? Welche Rolle kann das Marketing für eine mehr zielgruppenorientierte Gestaltung von Ausstellungen spielen? Welche Auswirkungen haben neue Formate auf die Ausstellungs- und Museumsarchitektur? Und welche Folgen bzw. welches Innovationspotenzial bringt der sicher weiter zunehmende Einsatz von Smartphones bzw. Tablets im Ausstellungswesen mit sich, etwa mittels *Augmented Reality*-Software?

Im Rahmen dieses Bandes können leider nur drei Vorträge des Symposiums dokumentiert werden, ergänzt jedoch um einen weiteren relevanten Beitrag von einer Lehrbeauftragten des Erlanger Instituts für Kunstgeschichte und Mitarbeiterin der Bayerischen Schlösserverwaltung, Uta Piereth. Sie hat gemeinsam mit Sebastian Karnatz das neue Burgerlebnismuseum Cadolzburg bei Nürnberg konzipiert und eine Reihe begleitender Lehrveranstaltungen für Masterstudierende unseres Instituts angeboten. Unter anderem erarbeiteten sie gemeinsam anhand von Graphikbeständen der UB Erlangen die Sonderausstellung „Fenster zum Hof: Graphische Einblicke in das höfische Leben von Dürer und Zeitgenossen", die im Rahmen der Museumseröffnung zu sehen war.

Die vier Beiträge des vorliegenden Bandes thematisieren unterschiedliche Aspekte von

Dauerausstellungen. Anne-Lise Desmas ist als *Senior Curator* am J. Paul Getty Museum in Los Angeles für die Abteilung *Sculpture and Decorative Arts* verantwortlich und schildert die Schwierigkeiten, die sich trotz der geradezu sagenhaften finanziellen Ressourcen dieses Museums bei dem Versuch ergeben, die vor rund zwanzig Jahren eingerichtete Dauerausstellung des Hauses behutsam zu modernisieren. Die Präsentation der Objekte war ursprünglich nicht auf Zuwachs angelegt; zudem bedingt das hohe Erdbebenrisiko der Region eine feste Verankerung der Skulpturen, was dem Wunsch nach einer flexiblen Neugestaltung nicht unerhebliche Hindernisse in den Weg legt. Die Entscheidung, Objekte in *period rooms* zu vereinen, die das Eintauchen in ein historisches Ambiente suggerieren, brachte den Nachteil mit sich, dass viele Objekte nur aus der Ferne und nicht unter optimalen Beleuchtungsverhältnissen gewürdigt werden können. Außerdem verhinderte die strikte Trennung der Departments eine kunsthistorisch sinnvolle Gegenüberstellung bestimmter Objekte. In Kooperation mit dem Kurator der Gemäldesammlung hat Anne-Lise Desmas in den letzten Jahren neue gattungsübergreifende Präsentationsformen entwickelt und neue Ausstellungsflächen erschlossen, wo Skulpturen und Kunsthandwerk angemessen zur Geltung kommen und bisher in den Depots verborgene Bestände gezeigt werden können. Zudem bespricht sie museumsdidaktische Verbesserungen unter Einbeziehung von Medienstationen.

Unter der Devise „Museumsbesucher zu Nutzern machen" erläutert Katarina Horst die Bemühungen des Badischen Landesmuseums in Karlsruhe, die Sammlungen dieses Hauses partizipativ zu erschließen. Sie erörtert zunächst die historischen Präsentationsformen am Badischen Landesmuseum, um dann auf die daraus resultierenden Desiderate einzugehen. Da im Jahr 2014 90% aller Besucher der elf Landesmuseen in Baden-Württemberg nur wegen der aktuellen Sonderausstellungen ins Museum kamen, ergibt sich die dringende Notwendigkeit, Dauerausstellungen für das Publikum attraktiver zu machen. Um dies zu erreichen, plant das Badische Landesmuseum die Realisierung von drei unterschiedlichen Präsentationsformaten. Im zentralen Teil des Schlosses soll ein Überblick über die Sammlung gegeben werden, der sich auf relativ wenige, besonders bedeutungsvolle Objekte konzentriert. Daneben werden mehrere, auf drei bis vier Jahre angelegte semipermanente Ausstellungen zu bestimmten aktuellen Themenschwerpunkten eingerichtet, und schließlich soll drittens ein großer Teil der Bestände in Schaudepots zugänglich gemacht werden. In der „Expothek" erhalten Museumsbesucher die Möglichkeit, über Smartphone oder Tablet Informationen zu den Exponaten abzurufen und Objekte zu bestellen, die sie dann in sogenannten „Oasen" näher in Augenschein nehmen können.

Während Anne-Lise Desmas und Katarina Horst über die Aktualisierung bereits bestehender Dauerausstellungen berichten, gibt Uta Piereth am Beispiel des im Juni 2017 eröffneten Erlebnismuseums Cadolzburg bei Nürnberg facettenreiche Einblicke in Konzeption und Realisation einer komplett neuen Dauerausstellung. Ausgangsbasis war die seit 1945 in ruinösem Zustand darniederliegende Burganlage, die seit 1979 baulich gesichert wurde und seit 2007 lediglich teilweise für Veranstaltungen genutzt werden konnte. Der Bayerischen

Schlösserverwaltung kam die Mammutaufgabe zu, in der Cadolzburg – einem der wichtigsten Herrschaftssitze des Hauses Hohenzollern – ein Burgerlebnismuseum einzurichten, das den Ort gleichsam aus dem Dornröschenschlaf der Geschichte wecken und möglichst bis über die Region hinaus neu im kulturellen Bewusstsein verankern sollte. Anliegen der Kuratoren Uta Piereth und Sebastian Karnatz war es, die Cadolzburg selbst zum primären Objekt der musealen Präsentation zu machen. Der zeitliche Fokus wurde auf das für die Hohenzollern schicksalsträchtige 15. Jahrhundert gelegt, in dem die Nürnberger Burggrafen zu Kurfürsten von Brandenburg aufstiegen. Das Ausstellungs- und Vermittlungskonzept verfolgt den Ansatz, bei den Besuchern Lust an selbstbestimmter, aktiver und teils auch gemeinschaftlicher Aneignung der Inhalte auf allen Ebenen zu fördern und dabei ein möglichst breites Publikum anzusprechen. Den Museumsgästen stehen hierzu unterschiedlichste, die verschiedenen Sinne ansprechende Angebote zur Verfügung, die einen auch zum Wiederbesuch der Cadolzburg reizenden „Kulturhunger" stimulieren.

Der vierte Beitrag von Matthias Henkel widmet sich dem Themenkomplex Ausstellungspraxis im digitalen Zeitalter. Welche Strategien können Museen für ihre Schausammlungen entwickeln, um auf die insbesondere durch die Digitalisierung forcierten Herausforderungen der Zukunft produktiv zu reagieren? Ausgehend von einem skizzenhaften Überblick über zentrale museologische Paradigmen, stellt Henkel Überlegungen zur zukünftigen Bedeutung der Institution Museum an und reflektiert insbesondere deren Wirkungsweise und Wirksamkeit sowie deren mögliche Potenziale und auch institutionelle Grenzen. An Praxisbeispielen werden die Chancen und Risiken beim Einsatz von *Social Media*-Plattformen wie Twitter, Facebook, Instagram und Co. vorgestellt. Themenbereiche wie Digitalisierung von Beständen, virtuelle Ausstellungen bzw. Rundgänge, Immersivität und *Augmented Reality* finden ebenfalls Berücksichtigung. Abgerundet wird Henkels Beitrag mit dem Versuch der Definition eines zeitgenössischen Instrumentariums, mit dem sich Museen auch in Zukunft am gesellschaftlichen Diskurs produktiv beteiligen können.

DANK

Ohne die tatkräftige Unterstützung zahlreicher Mitarbeiter/innen verschiedenster Museen und Institutionen wären unsere museologischen Initiativen nicht möglich gewesen. Die praxisbezogenen Sektionen des Studienkurses 2016 wurden am Germanischen Nationalmuseum von G. Ulrich Großmann, Daniel Hess und Oliver Mack geleitet; außerdem beteiligten sich Florian Dierl und Thomas Schauerte (Museen der Stadt Nürnberg), Nina Lutz (Geschichte für Alle e. V.) und Jessica Mack-Andrick (Kunst- und Kulturpädagogisches Zentrum der Museen in Nürnberg). Für das den Studienkurs ergänzende internationale Symposium konnten die folgenden Referent/inn/en gewonnen werden: Katharina Beisiegel (Art Centre Basel), Anne-Lise Desmas (J. Paul Getty Museum Los Angeles), Sibylle Ebert-Schifferer (Bibliotheca Hertziana – Max-Planck-Institut für Kunstgeschichte, Rom), Anja Grebe (Donau-Universität Krems), Matthias Henkel (Zentrum für *Audience Development* Berlin), Stephan Hoppe (Ludwig-Maximilians-Universität München) und Katarina Horst (Badisches Landesmuseum Karlsruhe).

Der Studienkurs 2017 wurde in kollegialer Zusammenarbeit mit Anselm Schubert (Lehrstuhl Kirchengeschichte II der Friedrich-Alexander-Universität Erlangen-Nürnberg) veranstaltet. Impulsreferate hielten Sebastian Karnatz und Uta Piereth (Bayerische Schlösserverwaltung), Thomas Schauerte (Museen der Stadt Nürnberg), Alexander Schubert (Historisches Museum der Pfalz Speyer) und Matthias Weniger (Bayerisches Nationalmuseum). Für Interviews und Diskussionen standen in den Museen die Kurator/inn/en und Beiräte der fünf besuchten Reformations-Jubiläumsausstellungen freundlich zur Verfügung: Thomas Eser (Germanisches Nationalmuseum), Fabian Fiederer und Peter Wolf (Haus der Bayerischen Geschichte), Benjamin Hasselhorn (Lutherhaus Wittenberg), Jutta Kraus (Wartburg-Stiftung Eisenach) und Elke Anna Werner (Freie Universität Berlin).

Maren Manzl und Siglinde Scholz haben Planung und Durchführung der beiden Studienkurse im Bereich Organisation tatkräftig unterstützt. Die sorgfältige Drucklegung und ansprechende Gestaltung dieses Bandes verdanken sich Michael Imhof und Patricia Koch. Das Lektorat übernahmen Sarah Lynch und Ulrike Rohde, unterstützt von Franziska Lorenz. Allen Genannten gilt unser herzlicher, aufrichtiger Dank.

Erlangen, im November 2018
Christina Strunck
Manuel Teget-Welz

Anne-Lise Desmas

DISPLAY CHOICES FOR THE SCULPTURE AND DECORATIVE ARTS COLLECTION AT THE J. PAUL GETTY MUSEUM

The J. Paul Getty Museum is named after its founder and benefactor, J. Paul Getty (Minneapolis, 1892–Surrey, 1976). Already a millionaire at twenty-three, he was declared the wealthiest businessman in the world by *Fortune* magazine in 1957, and his company, Getty Oil, was counted among the largest corporations in the world. His interest in art began early, with his first significant acquisitions dating to the 1930s. In 1948 he gave a few pieces to the Los Angeles County Museum of Art, and in 1953 he decided to establish his own museum in the ranch house he had bought in Malibu five years earlier. In 1953 the J. Paul Getty Museum Trust was established and from 1954 the collection was opened to the public twice a week. J. Paul Getty died in 1976, and most of his estate passed to the Trust in 1982, and its name legally changed to the J. Paul Getty Trust in 1983. Mr. Getty's philanthropy (he left the equivalent of three quarters of a billion dollars in today's standard for „the diffusion of artistic and general knowledge") enabled the construction of the Getty Villa in Pacific Palisades and the Getty Center in the Brentwood neighborhood of Los Angeles, the expansion of the Museum's collections, and the creation of three other institutions: the Getty Conservation Institute, the Getty Research Institute, and the Getty Foundation.

Contrary to many museums named after their founders, the Getty Museum collection as it is presented to visitors today in both the Getty Villa and the Getty Center has little to do with its benefactor. Surprisingly, it was only in 2016, on the occasion of the fortieth anniversary of Getty's bequest, that a gallery was devoted to the man, thanks to whom all the activities supported by the Getty Trust are possible. A permanent exhibition entitled *J. Paul Getty Life and Legacy* allows visitors to understand the personality, life, and interests of J. Paul Getty, as well as the history of both his collection and the institutions created after his death. In a gallery at the entrance to the South Pavilion, interactive screens offer layers of information next to a few artworks bought by Getty himself (fig. 1). An accompanying audio-guided tour provides the location of and comments on pieces purchased by Getty that are on view in the adjacent galleries.

At the time of J. Paul Getty's death in 1976, the collection of the museum was composed of objects he had acquired in his three favorite areas of interest: European decorative arts before 1800 (mostly, but not exclusively, French), antiquities, and European paintings. From 1982, the institution was able to broaden its collecting areas to include European sculpture, European drawings, illuminated manuscripts, and photographs with the creation, respectively, of four additional departments. These acquisitions, made intensively in the second half of the 1980s and in the 1990s, were focused on first-rate masterpieces, preferably in an excellent state of conservation, which was possible thanks to the extraordinary wealth of the J. Paul Getty Museum. Nonetheless, starting a collection at that date inevitably implied that in certain areas of the collection, it would be impossible to represent the totality of European art his-

Fig. 2 | South Pavilion, first floor, Rococo Paneled Room, about 1755 (unidentified Parisian paneled interior) [iPad on the Oeben table on the foreground]

Fig. 3 | South Pavilion, first floor, Neoclassical Paneled Room, about 1790-95 (main reception room of the house built for Jean-Baptiste Hosten in Place Vendôme by architect Claude Nicolas Ledoux)

Fig. 1 | South Pavilion, first floor, installation *J. Paul Getty Life and Legacy* (opened on Sept. 27, 2016, with didactic panels and interactive screens on the wall, and decorative art objects acquired by Getty under vitrines)

tory in a range of unique artefacts, and important areas remain underrepresented.

Until 2003, before the creation of the Department of Sculpture and Decorative Arts the following year, two distinct curatorial departments existed: one for French decorative arts led by curator Gillian Wilson, and another, the department of European Sculpture and Works of Art ('works of art' meaning in fact all the non-French decorative arts), led by Peter Fusco. Consequently, when the Getty Center was planned by architect Richard Meyer with its four pavilions (called North, South, East, and West) for the opening of the new Brentwood site in 1997, three departments had to organize the display of their respective collections in the permanent galleries: these two along with the Paintings department (the departments dealing exclusively with light-sensitive material were provided with galleries to organize rotating shows, while the Antiquities department could occupy the whole Getty Villa). Distinct spaces were allotted to these three departments, and almost no attempt was made to display works from separate departments together. The French decorative arts were given the entire first floor of the South Pavilion. A designer, Thierry Despont,

Fig. 4 | South Pavilion, first floor, first gallery with the comte de Toulouse Beauvais tapestry series of *The Story of the Emperor of China*, and Boulle pieces of furniture (designed by Thierry Despont, with a modern mirror and chimney, including an early 18th-century fire back that bears the arms of the comte de Toulouse)

Fig. 5 | South Pavilion, first floor, Boulle gallery (designed by Thierry Despont)

was hired for this part of the collection. In some instances, he created period rooms using the original wall paneling or hardwood floors that the museum had acquired (fig. 2-3). However, in the majority of the galleries, his scenography aimed at creating faux-period rooms in the style of the late-seventeenth or eighteenth centuries with the walls covered in tinted plaster or fine damasks, and with elaborate moldings, columns, false chimneys, and 'antique' hardwood floors (fig. 4-5 and plate I). In order to take advantage of the overhead light, the paintings were to be installed on the second floor of each pavilion (in a chronological sequence beginning in the North Pavilion and moving clockwise through the East, South, and West Pavilions), in galleries with a system of louvers moving up or down to filter the light depending on the time of the day. Sculpture and non-French decorative arts were given most of the first-floor galleries of the three remaining pavilions (fig. 6) (North, East, and West, chronologically). Most of the installations for the galleries were planned as if the collection would not grow significantly, leaving little, or even no flexibility for easily managed changes in the future. This same lack of flexibility also characterizes some later installations, such as the ground floor galleries in the North Pavilion. These galleries were renovated by Antonia Boström and included vitrines designed for specific groups of objects and walls with displays of stained glass pieces that were planned in such a way that none can be removed or added without the whole ensemble being compromised (fig. 7).

The collecting history and design choices of the galleries have a direct impact on the Getty Center's current display initiatives for the permanent collections, and in particular for those of sculpture and decorative arts. An additional factor defines the feasibility and flexibility of any plan for new installations: seismic faults, in particular the San Andreas fault, that run through California, which makes the risk of an earthquake a constant concern. Each piece must be securely mounted, sometimes with heavy and complex hardware. This prevents frequent relocations of the objects since this would require a great deal of effort as well as leaving numerous holes in the floors and walls of the galleries.

The decision to merge the French Decorative Arts Department and the Sculpture and Works of Art Department into a single Sculpture and Decorative Arts Department in 2004 was wise. Displaying sculpture and decorative arts together in the J. Paul Getty Museum makes art-historical sense; both these parts of the collection are rich in French eighteenth-century works. However, installing sculpture in the decorative arts galleries of the South Pavilion in order to recreate eighteenth-century interiors even more accurately, poses significant challenges for several reasons. Certain pieces, particularly works in terracotta, are very fragile and must be placed under vitrines: this means adding modern pedestals in proximity to eighteenth-century furniture and consequently breaking the aesthetic visual unity. The only exception in the Getty

Fig. 6 | East Pavilion, first floor, gallery on European Sculpture and Decorative Arts, 1600-1650 (in Richard Meyer's architecture, with the typical grey Venetian plaster walls)

Fig. 7 | North Pavilion, first floor, gallery on Sacred Art, 1150-1600 (installed in May 2010)

collection is the pair of bronze groups, *Pluto Abducting Proserpine* by Girardon and *Boreas Abducting Orithyia* after a model by Gaspard Marsy, which are beautifully installed without vitrines, thanks to their Boulle pedestals (fig. 8). In addition, because of the risk of earthquakes, all the pieces must be secured either with mounts or wax. It is naturally very difficult, if not to say impossible, to install works of art on top of pieces of furniture, especially if they incorporate marquetry and/or veneered wood in their upper parts.

In 2010, when the eighteenth-century French sculpture collection was removed from the West Pavilion (in order to create a gallery for nineteenth-century works) and needed a new home, I found a compromise in using a space that was not initially meant for displaying art. This space, the South Atrium, is in the heart of the South Pavilion and thus directly connected to decorative arts objects with which these fine terracotta heads and marble statuettes would have been displayed in eighteenth-century France (fig. 9). There were no practical or aesthetic issues in placing vitrines in this empty, travertine-tiled area, and daylight coming from the windows of the ceiling is ideal for viewing the sculptures. This kind of lighting would be impossible in the decorative arts galleries on account of their many light-sensitive objects and consequent low lighting.

In 2014, I was able to successfully incorporate certain sculptures within the decorative arts galleries. These were a group of medium-size French bronzes, which had previously been in storage or improperly displayed in a room with Italian bronzes, and which I installed on top of the long, magnificent cabinet attributed to Bernard II van Risenburgh. As one of the objects that dominates the great hall of the South Pavilion, this cabinet, which is so long that it is actually made in three sections (the total length is 4.70m), has a marble top that had always looked empty. The installation of the four bronzes on this surface not only allowed these pieces to be on view in a more appropriate setting but also returned the cabinet to its original function (in eighteenth-century France, such a cabinet would have been used to display bronzes and/or porcelains). This new display aesthetically transformed the whole gallery into a more balanced ensemble of objects and a more harmonious space (fig. 4, and 10).

The period rooms designed and planned by Thierry Despont and Gillian Wilson certainly do allow our visitors to feel as if they travel back in time to the eighteenth century. The down-side of this display is that viewing individual objects can sometimes be compromised. This is the reason why I have advocated for a new installation of a group of objects from the collection of sil-

Fig. 8 | South Pavilion, first floor, French Tapestry gallery (designed by Thierry Despont; with bronze groups on top of Boulle pedestals)

Fig. 9 | South Pavilion, first floor, South Atrium, eighteenth-century marble and terracotta sculptures (installed in August 2012)

ver. Until recently, masterpieces of French silver were scattered across various galleries of the South Pavilion, either in vitrines embedded in walls, as planned for the 1997 opening, or in free-standing cases added in the past years. Most of these objects were consequently not appreciated in the round, many of the displays were poorly lit, and the modern cases disrupted the overall aesthetic of the interior design. In addition, this collection of silver objects, although consisting of masterpieces, is relatively small. Dispersing the objects in this manner diminished the magnificence of the collection. The new, installation, completed in late August 2016, occupies a space in the South Terrace, which was not initially meant for such displays but is still beautifully designed entirely in Richard Meyer's style with a polished travertine floor, a single rough travertine wall surrounded that contrasts with the other, pure white walls, and a huge window (fig. 11). Using this space allowed a few works of sixteenth- and seventeenth-century German silver to be brought out of storage, as well as a pair of monumental Neoclassical tureens by the famous English silversmith Paul Storr. The latter works were among the first purchases of decorative arts made by J. Paul Getty in 1938, but they had never been part of the permanent display at the Getty Center. Additionally, works by one of the premier French silversmiths, François-Thomas Germain, could also be exhibited together in this space. The new display improves the viewing experience by encouraging close examination of all the objects. Needless to say, the medium of silver shines magnificently in the intense natural light that changes over the course of the day. Individual objects can be appreciated in all their splendor, notably a pair of mid eighteenth-century French painted bronze and silver figures carrying sugarcanes that may have belonged to Madame de Pompadour; an early seventeenth-century Genoese basin with scenes representing the life of Antony and Cleopatra; and a silver plaque of the Virgin of the Immaculate Conception with a lapis lazuli background by Natale Juvarra circa 1730-1740. The result of this display is so satisfactory that there is now an initiative to develop a similar display for our collection of French porcelains. Since 1997, our pieces have been on view in narrow and poorly-lit wall vitrines or on top of pieces of furniture in period rooms that allow only a glance from

Fig. 10 | South Pavilion, first floor, Hall (detail of fig. 4 showing the mounts securing the French bronze sculptures on top of the cabinet by Bernard II van Risenburgh)

Fig. 11 | South Pavilion, first floor, South Terrace, display of the European silver collection (installed in August 2016)

a far distance, while others remain in storage. An ambitious re-installation in a space devoted to this small but high-quality ensemble would render the objects more accessible to our visitors.

While the South Pavilion offers a unique experience to visitors who cannot travel to Europe to visit historical *hôtels particuliers* or castles in France and have only the Getty Center to feel as if transported to an eighteenth-century interior, the artworks displayed in these galleries can hardly be appreciated individually for their own unique character and quality. It is difficult to find a balance between a viewing experience of an accurate art-historical interior and a close examination of specific works. Some didactic components may help. 2015 marked the tercentenary anniversary of the death of Louis XIV, and on this occasion, I developed a didactic panel at the entrance of the South Pavilion featuring a genealogical tree of the French Royal family illustrated not with portraits of kings and queens but with artworks owned by the Getty that were previously in the French royal collection (fig. 12). On a few occasions, hopefully to be repeated more frequently in the future, interactives on screens installed in the galleries allow visitors to open pieces of furniture virtually. In one of the period rooms (fig. 2), an iPad demonstrates how our Oeben table can become a functional writing table thanks to its elaborate key system, and a few screens surrounding our Augsburg cabinet give visitors the virtual possibility to open drawers and compartments with zooming function to appreciate its details, while the piece stands in front of them behind a railing (fig. 13). In addition, these interactives are accessible online in case visitors want to deepen their experience at home. These virtual experiences can be complemented with rare occasions when my curator colleagues open pieces of furniture during tours for visitors.

One must acknowledge that independently from the nature of a museum's overall collection, display initiatives often depend on the collegial collaboration that may or may not exist between curators of separate departments or institutions. Since the fall of 2010, thanks to the generosity of the Getty Research Institute, which has a rich collection of prints, and a team effort between curators of the Special Collections Curatorial Department and those of the Sculpture and Decorative Arts Department, it has been possible to hang framed engravings on the walls of one of the ground floor West Pavilion galleries (fig. 14). Indeed, in this gallery devoted to European sculpture and decorative arts in the late eighteenth-century, the presence of engravings, whose selection rotates every few months on account of these artworks' sensitivity to light, creates a meaningful display and shows how stylistic components and design tendencies can be found in a variety of artefacts including sculpture, small porcelains, tables and daybeds, and engravings, and could circulate throughout Europe via prints.

Since the arrival of Davide Gasparotto as Senior Curator of Paintings, we have been able to collaborate on new installations that mix sculptures and paintings together in the permanent galleries in order to reshape and refresh some of the displays in our respective collections. In 2015, while a new arrangement of paintings was being planned for the second-floor galleries in the North Pavilion, some sculptures were installed in these rooms. These included Giambologna's marble *Female Figure*, whose previous display in front of an off-white travertine wall was unsatisfactory. This work instead took its place upstairs in the room with red velvet wall coverings where Dosso Dossi's *Allegory of Fortune* and Titian's *Venus and Adonis* hang (fig. 15-16). Such juxtapositions of Renaissance masterpieces depicting nude female bodies enhance the aesthetic and stylistic viewing experience and encourage comparisons. However, as explained above, the upper galleries were meant initially to house only paintings. Consequently, if the back of Giambologna's statue is very well lit by the louvered skylight, the face of the figure and the front of the body are harder to read at certain times of the day, and no light fixture can correct this. The same lighting issue is true for the bronze *Double Head* attributed to Primaticcio, which is displayed on top of a column in the adjacent gallery. A whole electrical system should be planned to run just above the doors in order to add the possibility of side lighting to complement the overhead source.

For two recent sculpture acquisitions, the decision to display them in the paintings galleries was quite straightforward. The display of Rodin's group of *Christ and Mary Magdalene* in the Impressionists gallery next to paintings by artists with whom Rodin was friends or with whom he exhibited in Paris enhances the viewing experience in ways that would have been impossible had the group been installed on the ground floor galleries (fig. 17). On the occasion of the acquisition of the *Bust of Paul V* by Gian Lorenzo Bernini in 2015, a wall of the Italian Baroque paintings gallery was entirely re-

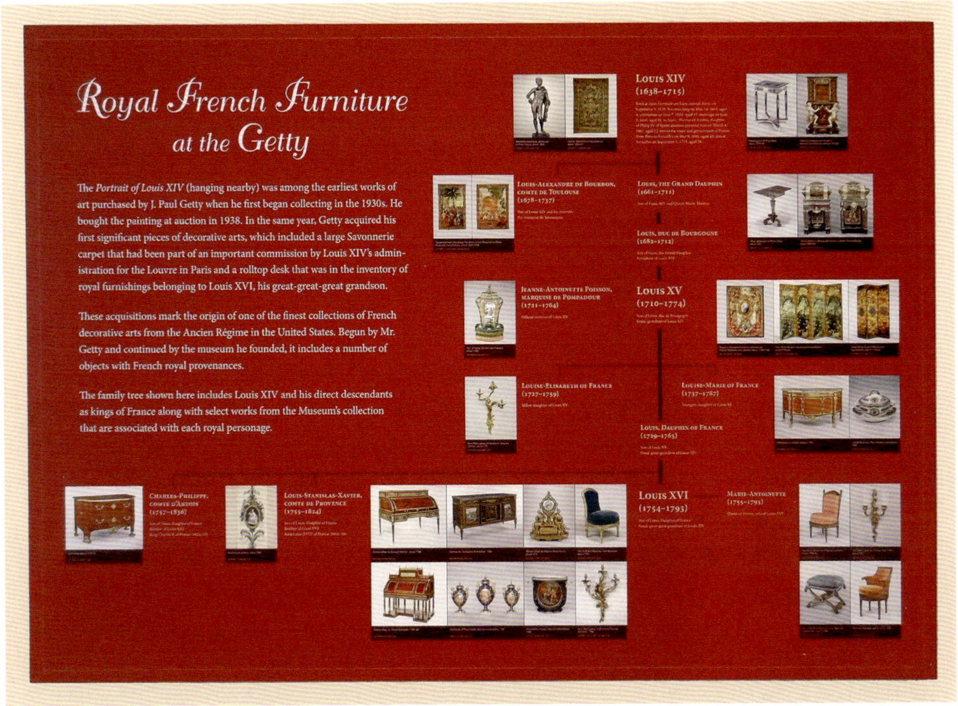

Fig. 12 | South Pavilion, entrance to first floor, didactic panel on Royal French Furniture at the Getty with a genealogy tree of kings and queens of France illustrated with Getty art objects they owned (hung since 2015, which marked the tercentenary of the death of Louis XIV)

configured; visitors are now presented with a unique ensemble of masterpieces of the art of portraiture in seventeenth-century Italy (fig. 18). In contrast, the display of the Borghese-Windsor cabinet, which I acquired in September 2016, presented difficulties. This remarkable piece of furniture, which is decorated with the coat of arms of Pope Paul V and was made in Rome in the early seventeenth-century, could legitimately be placed in the same gallery. However, on account of the cabinet's size, it would take up too much space and necessitate the removal of canvases that could not be exhibited elsewhere. Consequently, it will be installed on the ground floor of the East Pavilion with other works of sculpture and decorative arts in galleries that I plan to redesign in the future. Indeed, difficulties in displaying the growing collection have become increasingly frequent in Richard Meyer's 1997 building.

In some galleries, where paintings are quite frequently re-hung on account of works lent to and returning from outside exhibitions, the presence of sculptures can create difficulties. Indeed, because the pedestals have to be anchored to the floor (as an anti-seismic measure), the placement of busts or statues imposes constraints on the display of paintings; the constant rotation of paintings can result in unsuccessful juxtapositions between artworks when new paintings have to replace outgoing loans.

Nonetheless, Davide Gasparotto and I try as much as possible to create displays that incorporate paintings and sculptures from the same period together, in order to create ensembles that are aesthetically pleasing and art-historically meaningful. This also allows us to get around some of the weaknesses and gaps in the museum's collection. In the near future, in one of the West Pavilion ground floor galleries devoted to nineteenth-century and early-twentieth-century sculpture where no paintings are currently hung, a group of canvases by Joaquín Sorolla y Bastida (possibly with other works) will be included in the new display. At the same time, some of the sculptures by Constantin Meunier, George Minne, and others, will be transferred to the gallery on the second floor, called the Ensor gallery because of the large painting *Christ's Entry to Brussels in 1889*.

In contrast, there are galleries in which mixing paintings and sculptures would not be appropriate (fig. 19-20 and plate II). This is particularly the case in the Neoclassical gallery on the ground floor of the West Pavilion because of the nature of the sculpture collection for this period. Among the European schools represented, the English pieces form a distinctive group because of their size, number and quality, and above all because of their provenance. Indeed,

Fig. 13 | North Pavilion, first floor, gallery on Collecting in Northern Europe, 1450-1600 (installed in May 2010; with the Augsburg cabinet in the middle and the interactive screen about this object)

Fig. 14 | West Pavilion, first floor, gallery on Neoclassical Decorative Arts (with prints on loan from the Getty Research Institute on the walls)

the J. Paul Getty Museum owns no fewer than nine sculptures all formerly in the collection of Charles Watson-Wentworth, second Marquess of Rockingham (1730–1782), one of the most avid and interesting collectors of sculpture in Britain in the eighteenth century. At the opening of the Getty Center in 1997, only the three statues of goddesses by Joseph Nollekens (*Venus*, *Minerva* and *Juno*), and the two busts of philosophers by Joseph Wilton were included in the display. For the re-installation of the first floor of the West Pavilion in September 2010 (after it was emptied to host the exhibition *Leonardo and the Art of Sculpture*), two statuettes, *Isis* and *Apollo Belvedere*, attributed to Wilton's workshop, were taken out of storage and exhibited together with the above mentioned five sculptures. These statuettes had not been initially included because of their condition (some fingers are missing). However, it is quite meaningful to exhibit them considering the importance of such reproductions after famous ancient statues in both the history of collecting and the history of sculpture in eighteenth-century Britain. Nonetheless, their addition to the gallery was not sufficient, as I also wanted to incorporate the other two pieces belonging to the Lord Rockingham's collection: the statue of *Paris* and the relief of the *Triumph of Bacchus*. The new installation in the Neoclassical gallery was completed in 2013, and the display now evokes the taste and modality of collecting of an eighteenth-century British Grand Tourist.

In a 1991 article in the *J. Paul Getty Museum Journal* about Lord Rockingham's collection, Nicholas Penny stated: "*The Judg-*

ment of Paris is one of Nollekens's finest works. It is also one of the most ambitious narrative groups ever created by an English sculptor. Moreover, it is a composition of a most unusual kind, with the figures interacting across a considerable space, and one of its components is an ancient work – or rather a work that in part purports to be ancient." It is actually thanks to Nicholas Penny's acumen that the four statues forming this group (the three Nollekens' *Goddesses* and the ancient *Paris* statue) were assembled by the same dealer and then, in 1987, acquired together by the J. Paul Getty Museum. Indeed, Nicholas Penny had published a letter on July 4, 1986, in the London *Times*, to point out that the four statues, though offered in separate lots by Christie's in preparation for the sale of Wentworth Woodhouse's collection, formed a unique group. In response to this, Christie's displayed the statues in the same room and drew the attention of bidders to the relationship between them. However, since the acquisition of the statues by the museum in 1987, they have never been displayed together. Indeed, the *Paris* statue has been kept in storage most of the time

Fig. 15 | J. Paul Getty Museum, North Pavilion, second floor, Renaissance Painting galleries (with Giambologna's marble *Female Figure* in the center and Titian's *Venus and Adonis* at right, Primaticcio's bronze *Double Head* in the background)

Fig. 16 | J. Paul Getty Museum, North Pavilion, second floor, Italian Renaissance Painting gallery (with Giambologna's *Female Figure* in the center, Titian's *Venus and Adonis* at left, Dossi's *Allegory of Fortune* at right, and zenithal lighting through louvers)

and exhibited only for the small *Dilettanti* exhibition at the Getty Villa in 2008. Indeed, its patchwork appearance, its yellowish color, and its heavy restorations in the seventeenth century had prevented *Paris* from being exhibited next to the pure white marble and perfectly conserved statues of the *Goddesses*. Nevertheless, the statue was granted consideration in the eighteenth century as an antique, not only by Lord Rockingham, but also its previous owner, Lyde Browne. Artists were interested in the statue and copied it, as testified by two drawings, one of which is by Giovanni Battista Cipriani, the sculptor who signed the two bronzes of *Venus* and *Dancing Faun*, acquired by the Getty in 2008. More importantly perhaps, the statue was published by Winckelmann in his *Monumenti antichi inediti* of 1767, with the proposal – still valid today – that it had been wrongly restored and did not in fact originally represent the shepherd Paris but a young priest. The year 1767 serves therefore as a *terminus ante quem* date for the restorations of the statue. Last but not least, a new study by Claudio Pizzorusso has just revealed that the inscription on the back of the statue (the number 48 followed by the initials I. B.) may indicate that the restorations were made by Ippolito Buzio when the piece most likely was part of the Ludovisi collection. Certainly, without *Paris*, the extraordinary narrative of the group that Nollekens created to accompany the statue is completely lost; displaying the four statues together re-creates the ensemble as an eighteenth-century collector of the highest rank and one of the best eighteenth-century British sculptors conceived it.

While the abovementioned sculptures were acquired in 1987 by the J. Paul Getty Museum, after the 1986 Wentworth Woodhouse sale, there was already at the Getty Villa a piece from Lord Rockingham's collection, a marble relief purchased by J. Paul Getty in 1953, a few years after the first sale of the same estate in 1949. Like the *Paris* statue, the relief was exhibited in the *Dilettanti* exhibition in 2008 but had otherwise been kept in storage at the Getty Villa, due to its significant restorations. The provenance of this relief is nonetheless very important for the history of the taste for the antique in the eighteenth century. Discovered in Rome between 1728 and 1730, it belonged to Cardinal de Polignac, the French ambassador in Italy, who conducted many excavations during his tenure there. Polignac was one of the key society figures in the collectors' and antiquarians' circle in Rome. The relief, with the cardinal's collection, was then brought to Paris in 1731, and at the cardinal's death in 1741 it was given to the sculptor Lambert-Sigisbert Adam as partial payment for work he had done for Polignac. Adam, one of the most important French sculptors of the first half of the eighteenth century, began working for the car-

Fig. 17 | West Pavilion, second floor, Impressionism gallery (with Rodin's *Christ and Mary Magdalene* installed in March 2015, and zenithal lighting through louvers)

Fig. 18 | East Pavilion, second floor, Italian Baroque Painting gallery (wall installed in June 2015, with Fetti's *Portrait of a Man*, Van Dyck's *Portrait of Agostino Pallavicini*, Bernini's *Bust of Paul V*, and Guercino's *Portrait of Gregory XV*)

dinal as a restorer of antiquities when he was a *pensionnaire* at the French Academy in Rome. In 1755, Adam published a *Recueil* of the ancient sculptures in his atelier, most of them from Polignac's collection, with the intention of selling these objects (a copy of this *Recueil* is in the Special Collections of the Getty Research Institute). The engravings were made after his own drawings of the objects and included the objects' titles and dimensions. The relief appears on plate four of this *Recueil* and includes all the restorations done by Lambert-Sigisbert Adam (this engraving is reproduced on the gallery label). The relief stayed in Adam's collection until his death in 1759 and was sold in 1763 or 1764 when the sculptor's estate was dispersed. It was most likely purchased at that time by Lord Rockingham. The restorations made by Adam are clearly visible, but they are also what makes the relief particularly intriguing. One can easily distinguish the ancient head of the man lying under the elephant from the modern heads carved by Adam.

The addition of the *Triumph of Bacchus* relief and the *Paris* statue in the Neoclassical gallery enabled, for the first time since their dispersal, an unprecedented display of all the sculptures from Lord Rockingham's collection owned by the J. Paul Getty Museum. This display perfectly reflects the arrangement of an elite, eighteenth-century British sculpture gallery (that is, without paintings but with busts, statues, and reliefs, either antique or made in the eighteenth century). Moreover, they offer a unique experience for the public in viewing and understanding the taste for and perception of ancient art in the eighteenth century as well as the ways in which restorations were handled in this period.

Far from aiming for an exhaustive presentation, the examples I have selected for this paper highlight the challenges of installing artworks in the permanent galleries. A Museum imposes many constraints on display choices due to its particular history, the nature of its collection, its location and audience, and its key staff members. In addition, the management of the permanent collections suffers from the fact that museums are increasingly exhibition driven. To the fullest extent possible, the new directions I have proposed and continue to plan in terms of display have been motivated by the desire to remove artworks from storage or from locations where they could not be fully appreciated, and to offer a viewing experience that is historically and stylistically meaningful as well as aesthetically well balanced. Last but not least, it is always critical to take into consideration the fluctuating state of the collection (the result of objects being sent on loans and others being borrowed or acquired) and the opportunity for multi-layered interpretations. Consequently, planning flexible installations that can be easily changed and adapted to new and un-

Fig. 19 | West Pavilion, first floor, Neoclassical Sculpture gallery, wall with the two busts of philosophers by Joseph Wilton and the statuette of *Isis* and *Apollo Belvedere* by Wilton's workshop (which belonged to Lord Rockingham)

Fig. 20 | West Pavilion, first floor, Neoclassical Sculpture gallery, group of *The Judgement of Paris* and in the background, ancient relief of *The Triumph of Bacchus* installed in October 2013 (all belonged to Lord Rockingham)

expected needs, and complementing them with digital tools and content that modern technology continues to improve plays a key role in the success of display initiatives. Nonetheless, presenting appropriate displays of a growing collection in a museum whose installation design was defined twenty years ago with rigid criteria becomes increasingly challenging. It is to be hoped that the approaching twenty-fifth anniversary of the opening of the Getty Center in 2022 may soon offer the possibility of completely reevaluating the display of the permanent collections galleries.

Plate I, p. 36-37 | South Pavilion, first floor, Hall (designed by Thierry Despont; on the left, cabinet by Bernard II van Risenburgh – with French bronze sculptures installed on top of it in 2014 –, in the middle, double desk by the same cabinet maker)

Plate II, p. 38-39 | West Pavilion, first floor, Neoclassical Sculpture gallery (general view including the sculptures mentioned in fig. 20, and in addition, Canova's *Apollo Crowing Himself*, Cipriani's *Venus and Dancing Faun*, and Cavaceppi's *Bust of Caracalla*)

Katarina Horst

MUSEUMSBESUCHER ZU NUTZERN MACHEN – DIE NEUKONZEPTION DES BADISCHEN LANDESMUSEUMS

EINLEITUNG

Eine dringende und komplette Sanierung des Karlsruher Schlosses ermöglicht die Chance, ein neues zukunftsweisendes Einrichtungskonzept zu realisieren, das vor allem die Dauereinrichtung in den Fokus setzt: jedes Sammlungsobjekt für alle Bürger[1] öffentlich zugänglich zu machen wie in einem Archiv. In der „Expothek" können sich die Nutzer einzelne Objekte bestellen, um sich damit näher zu befassen. Nutzerorientierte Orte, sogenannte Oasen, können zu verschiedenen Anlässen und Zwecken gebucht werden. So wird das Museum zu einem offenen Ort, an dem kulturelle Identitäten vermittelt und aktuelle Fragen der Gegenwart verhandelt werden.

Jedes Museum ist ein komplexer Organismus, ist das Ergebnis menschlichen Tuns über viele Jahre und Jahrzehnte. Dadurch ist jedes Museum unterschiedlich, ver-

Abb. 1 | Karlsruher Schloss

gleichbar mit den Individuen dieser Welt. Und wie jedes Individuum stellt sich auch jedes Museum die Fragen: Woher komme ich? Wer bin ich? Und wo will ich hin? So auch das Badische Landesmuseum in Karlsruhe (Abb. 1).

Bevor ich auf die letzte Frage – also: wo wollen wir hin? – eingehe, widme ich mich den ersten beiden Fragen, denn deren Ergebnisse bilden die Basis für die Beantwortung der letzte Frage.

1. WOHER KOMME ICH?

Es ist die Frage nach der Entstehungs- und Entwicklungsgeschichte des Badischen Landesmuseums, die ich hier in groben Zügen darstellen möchte. Stichtag für die Gründung eines Museums in Karlsruhe war der 12. Juli 1837. Großherzog Leopold von Baden beschloss gemeinsam mit den Volksvertretern, eine Sammlung von Antiken und von Gemälden aufzubauen und dafür einen Museumsbau zu realisieren. In dieses Museum sollten auch die bis dato gesammelten Kunstobjekte des Großherzogs Eingang finden, also die Objekte der Kunst- und Wunderkammer und die zahlreichen Gemälde. Die Idee, eine öffentliche museale Anstalt einzurichten, die sowohl den Gewerbeschaffenden und den Künstlern als auch dem gemeinen Volke zugänglich gemacht werden sollte, war zu diesem Zeitpunkt nichts aufregend Neues. Gerade erst waren die großen Vorbilder in Berlin (Altes Museum) und in München (Glyptothek und Pinakothek) eröffnet worden, ganz zu schweigen von der frühen Gründung des Fridericianums in Kassel. Da wollte Karlsruhe nicht nachstehen, aber entsprechend

Abb. 2 | Kunsthalle Karlsruhe, 1859

Abb. 3 | Querschnitt durch die Kunsthalle Karlsruhe, 1937

seiner Größe und Bedeutung in der politischen Landschaft wurde das Museum kleiner und bescheidener in der Ausführung. Es entstand 1848 der erste Museumsbau in Karlsruhe, der heute noch vorhanden ist und noch denselben Namen trägt: „Kunsthalle" (Abb. 2).

Der badische Rittmeister Friedrich Maler wurde als Kunstagent nach Rom entsandt mit der Vorgabe, antike Vasen und Terrakotten für das neue Museum zu erwerben, was ihm gelang. Darüber hinaus kaufte er aus eigenen Mitteln eine Sammlung hervorragender etruskischer und griechischer Bronzen, die einige Jahre später vom Karlsruher Museum übernommen wurde. Die Erwerbungen Malers bilden den Grundstock der Antikensammlung, weitere Ankäufe vor allem von Privatsammlungen vergrößerten allmählich den Bestand. Gleichzeitig mit den Antiken wurden Gipsabgüsse von antiken Statuen erworben. Die Gemäldesammlung, die durch die Sammelleidenschaft der Markgräfin Caroline Luise schon im 18. Jahrhundert einen hervorragenden Bestand vorweisen konnte, zog nun ebenfalls in den Neubau der Kunsthalle ein.

Ein kolorierter Stich aus den Händen des Kunsthallenarchitekten Heinrich Hübsch zeigt, wie die Aufteilung des Museums geplant war (Abb. 3): Im Erdgeschoss befanden sich die Antiken (auf Konsolen und Tischen frei präsentiert) zusammen mit den Gipsabgüssen, das obere Stockwerk nahm die Gemäldegalerie ein. Schon in der Planungsphase war angedacht, dass die Dekoration der Wände auf die Aufstellung Rücksicht nehmen sollte: In den oberen Raumteilen der Antikenhallen finden sich u.a. Wandfriese mit Nachempfindungen nach griechischen Vasen- und Reliefbildern.

Die Sammlung wuchs stetig und schnell, das Kunsthallengebäude wurde zu klein, und so realisierte man bereits 1875 einen weiteren Museumsbau, diesmal südwestlich des Marktplatzes am Friedrichsplatz. In dieses große Gebäude wurde die Antikensammlung umgesiedelt (Abb. 4).

Zusätzlich wurden dort andere Sammlungen zusammengetragen, die bisher an verschiedenen Orten aufbewahrt worden waren, so die Sammlung der sogenannten „vaterländischen Altertümer", also die ur- und frühgeschichtlichen und provinzialrömischen Sammlungen Badens sowie die naturkundliche Sammlung. Der erste Kurator, Ernst Wagner, verdient noch heute unseren Respekt und Dank für die komplette Inventarisierung der bis dato vorhandenen Objekte. Auch setzte er sich dafür ein, dass das Museum als Volksbildungsstätte „für Gebildete und Ungebildete offen steht [...] und die Teilnahme aller möglich [sein soll], auch der niedrigen Klassen unserer Bevölkerung am geistigen Gut, am befreienden Wissen so wie am Genuß des Schönen in der Kunst".[2]

Nach dem Ersten Weltkrieg, dem Zusammenbruch des deutschen Kaiserreichs und der Abdankung der regierenden Adeligen in Deutschland, also auch des Großherzogs von Baden 1918, wurde eine neue „Immobilie" (neudeutsch) frei, nämlich das Residenzschloss der badischen Familie (Abb. 1).

Und wieder gab es einen Umzug von Sammlungskonglomeraten: Alle Antiken aus dem Friedrichsbau und nun zusätzlich die zahlreichen Artefakte der Kunst- und Gewerbeschule wurden ins Schloss umge-

Abb. 4 | Antikensaal im Museum am Friedrichsplatz in Karlsruhe

Abb. 5 | Karlsruher Schloss, Saal mit antiken Bronzen, nach 1919

siedelt, und dieses neue Museum wurde unter dem Namen Badisches Landesmuseum gegründet. Dies war nun der hoffentlich letzte Umzug, so dass heute die ehemaligen großherzoglichen Sammlungen auf drei Standorte in Karlsruhe verteilt sind: Die Kunsthalle beherbergt als Gemäldegalerie die Malerei und einige Gipsabgüsse, der Friedrichsbau die Naturalia unter dem Namen Staatliches Museum für Naturkunde, und im Schloss befindet sich das Badische Landesmuseum als kunst- und kulturgeschichtliches Museum.

Nach dem Umzug ins Schloss wurden die Objekte ihrer Kulturzugehörigkeit nach geordnet und dann chronologisch aufgereiht und zumeist in Vitrinen präsentiert. Einen Bezug auf die ehemalige Nutzung der Räume konnte es nicht geben, denn die Räume waren für andere Zwecke angelegt worden. 25 Jahre war die Sammlung so zu sehen (Abb. 5).

Unter dem Bombardement der Alliierten im Zweiten Weltkrieg wurde der Großteil der Sammlung in Salzminen im nahen Schwarzwald ausgelagert, eine im Nachhinein vernünftige Maßnahme, denn am 27. September 1944 fielen drei Brandbomben auf das Schloss und ließen den herrlichen Bau abbrennen, nur die steinerne Außenfassade blieb stehen.

Beim Wiederaufbau entschloss man sich, die alte Fassade wiederherzustellen, jedoch beim Innenausbau nicht der ehemaligen kleinteiligen Zimmeraufteilung des barocken Schlosses zu folgen, sondern – dem Zeitgeschmack der 1960er Jahre entsprechend – große Hallen mit wenigen Innenwänden und Stützen zu realisieren (Abb. 6). Diese großen Räume erlaubten nun eine ganz neue Präsentation der Sammlung: wenige ausgesuchte Objekte, die von hoher Kunstfertigkeit zeugten, wurden auf Podesten z.T. völlig frei aufgestellt. Wir würden das heute als „Highlight"-Show bezeichnen. Eine spärliche Beschriftung fand – wenn überhaupt – nur auf wenigen Schildchen statt. Diese Präsentationsform sollte hauptsächlich das gebildete Bürgertum erfreuen.

Mit der ersten Finanzkrise in den 1980er Jahren fand ein Umdenken in der Museumslandschaft statt, die just mit einer weiteren Umbauphase im Schloss einherging. Zum ersten Mal wurden auch Eintrittsgelder erhoben. Nun sollte nicht nur der vorgebildete und kunstliebende Bürger erfreut werden, sondern die breite Bevölkerung wurde wieder in den Fokus genommen, und dieser sollte und musste ja alles erklärt werden. In dieser „Erklärungswut" kam es zu den stark inszenierten Präsentationen

Abb. 6 | Antikensaal im Karlsruher Schloss, nach 1966

Abb. 7 | Antikensaal im Karlsruher Schloss, nach 1996. Foto: Thomas Goldschmidt, Badisches Landesmuseum

mit einer erhöhten Anzahl von Texttafeln jeden Formats und Anspruchs (Abb. 7). Dies ist nun die Ausgangslage für die Neukonzeption.

Bereits vor einigen Jahren wurde dem Badischen Landesmuseum vom Landesbetrieb für Vermögen und Bau des Landes Baden-Württemberg mitgeteilt, dass das Schloss sich einer umfangreichen Sanierung unterziehen müsse. Die in den 1960er Jahren eingebrachten Materialien folgen lange nicht mehr den Vorgaben für öffentliche Gebäude, die technischen und sanitären Anlagen sind überaltert und entsprechen nicht den modernen Standards. Mit dem Bauamt sind wir in enge Kooperation getreten, um die Planung des Umbaus vorzunehmen. Basis für die Planung ist die Beantwortung weiterer Fragen, z.B.: Was wollen wir denn präsentieren, in welchen Räumen? Und wie? Welche Funktionen ordnen wir den Räumen zu? Reicht der vorhandene Bau aus, um allen modernen Anforderungen eines Museums zu genügen? Die Planung, die Umsetzung, der Umbau und die Wiedereinrichtung bedeuten für uns eine gewaltige Arbeitsleistung, aber es ist eine ganz große Chance, etwas Neues zu kreieren, und das spornt uns alle an.

Was sollte man nun ändern, was behalten oder was neu machen?

Ich möchte hier die Worte unserer Referatsleiterin im Ministerium für Wissenschaft, Forschung und Kunst des Landes Baden-Württemberg zitieren, die sie 2015 im Rahmen einer Direktorenkonferenz sprach: „Alle elf Landesmuseen des Landes Baden-Württemberg hatten im Jahr 2014 insgesamt eine Million Besucher, dabei fielen 90 % der Besucher auf Sonderausstellungen und 10 % auf die Dauereinrichtungen. Meine Damen und Herren, Sie haben ein echtes Problem, Ihre Sammlungen an den Bürger zu bringen." Sie hatte uns deutlich vermittelt: Die Sonderausstellungen erwecken das Interesse einer großen Zahl von Menschen, aber die Sammlungsausstellungen nicht. Hier müssen wir ansetzen mit unserem Neukonzept.

2015 haben wir mit der Arbeit an der Einrichtungskonzeption begonnen. Erster Schritt war die Gründung interner Arbeitskreise. Von denen möchte ich nur die hier relevanten nennen, nämlich den Arbeitskreis „digitale Strategie" und den Arbeitskreis „inhaltliches Konzept". Der letztgenannte bestand aus den 15 festangestellten Kuratoren. Intern bezeichnen wir diese Gruppe als „think tank". Doch bevor wir uns an eine inhaltliche und räumliche Aufteilung machten, war uns ein Exkurs wichtig, nämlich die Beantwortung der zweiten Frage:

2. WER BIN ICH?

Wir formulierten folgende Kernaussagen zum Thema Museum. Dies sind quasi die sechs Gebote, die zur Basis für das Konzept wurden:

- Museen haben ein Alleinstellungsmerkmal, nämlich: Das Museum ist der Ort der Originale.
- Das Museum ist wertvoll: wert-voll, voller Werte. Diese sind nicht nur pekuniär gemeint, sondern auch gesellschaftlich und emotional.
- Das Museum ist ein sozialer Raum, ein Kulturraum mit allen und für alle.
- Das Museum hat gesellschaftliche Relevanz: es ist ein Ort der Glaubwürdigkeit und hat somit Stabilisierungscharakter für die Gesellschaft.
- Das Museum ist Spiegel der Gesellschaft: Verändert sich die Gesellschaft, so muss sich auch das Museum ändern. Aktuelle gesellschaftliche und politische Themen müssen sich im Museum wiederfinden.
- Das Museum ist ein Ort des Dialogs: Im Museum kommen Menschen zusammen, um sich mit anderen Menschen auszutauschen. Das Museum darf nicht harmonisieren, sondern muss sich schwieriger Themen annehmen. Dissens ist eine hervorragende Vorgabe für das Entstehen von Dialogen und Gesprächsrunden.

Der Erhalt dieses Wertekanons ist von oberster Priorität. Er bildet die Voraussetzung unseres Arbeitens im Museum.

3. WO WILL ICH HIN?

Wie oben kurz angerissen, haben wir große Erfolge in der Veranstaltung von Sonderausstellungen. Sie waren in den letzten 20 bis 30 Jahren *die* Publikumsmagneten. Daher werden wir dieses Format nicht aufgeben, im Gegenteil: Wir möchten die Sonderausstellungen noch weiter ausbauen, indem wir ihnen mehr Platz im Schloss einräumen. Bisher ist der Sonderausstellungssaal im Erdgeschoss des Ostflügels untergebracht und verfügt über nahezu 1000 qm.

Die großen Stützwände teilen den großen Raum in Abschnitte, die je nach Bedarf teilweise oder ganz bespielt werden. Oft wurde der letzte östliche Abschnitt, der 150 qm ausmacht, als museumspädagogischer Aktionsraum genutzt. Dort können – passend zum Ausstellungsthema – praktische Arbeiten durchgeführt werden oder Abendveranstaltungen stattfinden, u. a. weil eine große Tür nach außen auf den Schlossplatz sowie eigene Toilettenräume vorhanden sind. Aus diesen Gründen dient dieser Bereich auch als Auspackraum in der Aufbauphase.

In der Planung ist vorgesehen, nun auch den Saal im ersten Stockwerk genau darüber als Raum für Sonderausstellungen zu nutzen. Hier sind z.Z. die Sammlungsausstellungen Barock und Absolutismus, Kunst- und Wunderkammer, Waffenkammer und die sogenannte Türkenbeute untergebracht. Sonderausstellungen verlangen aber nicht nur Räume für die Präsentationen selbst. Eine ausgereifte Organisation, Logistik und ausreichend Platz sind für den Aufbau der Einrichtung erforderlich. Problematisch ist, dass bisher diese Arbeiten wie auch das Auspacken der Objekte in den Ausstellungsräumen selber stattfinden müssen. Nun möchten wir diese Logistik im wahrsten Sinn der Worte „unter die Erde bringen“: Dafür möchten wir die Ostterrasse unterkellern und in den so entstandenen Räumlichkeiten den Auspackraum und die Werkstätten unterbringen. Eine hier einzubauende Verladerampe würde es möglich machen, dass die Objektkisten direkt in die Räumlichkeiten eingeliefert werden. Nach dem Auspacken, Prüfen und ggf. Restaurieren der Objekte können diese durch den bereits vorhandenen Lastenaufzug in die Ausstellungsräume gebracht werden.

KERNSTÜCK DES NEUEN KONZEPTS: DIE EINRICHTUNG DER SAMMLUNGSAUSSTELLUNGEN

Bisher sind die Sammlungen nach einer chronologisch-thematischen Konzeption eingerichtet worden, beginnend im Untergeschoss mit der Steinzeit und in die oberen Stockwerke hinein zeitlich abfolgend bis in das 20. Jahrhundert. Prinzipiell soll sich dies nicht ändern, es wird weiterhin eine chronologische Abfolge geben.

Den Auftakt in die permanente Ausstellungseinheit im Erdgeschoss bildet ein Prolog, der sowohl inhaltlich als auch optisch/ästhetisch auf den Besuch einstimmt. In einer Art Setzkasten (modern und transparent) findet der Besucher eine Zusammenstellung von Objekten, die er dann in allen drei Teilen der Sammlungsausstellung, die sich auf drei Stockwerke erstreckt, wiederfindet. Der Setzkasten vermittelt bildlich die Idee des „Sammelns von Dingen“ (ein Ur-Instinkt des Menschen) und „Die Sammlung des Badischen Landesmuseums“. Diesem Prolog geben wir den Namen „Die Welt in Baden“.

Die gesamte Sammlungsausstellung erhält den Namen „Baden und die Welt“. Im Erdgeschoss wird die Antike präsentiert, im ersten Obergeschoss das Mittelalter und die Neuzeit bis 1800, und im zweiten Obergeschoss findet man die Epoche von 1800 bis heute bzw. morgen, denn hier muss genügend Platz für die wachsende Sammlung der Zukunft eingeplant werden.

Das Wesentliche dieses Plans aber ist: Die Sammlungen werden in drei unterschiedliche Präsentationsformate unterteilt. Format 1 ist die noch immer konservative Präsentation der permanenten Sammlung, aber nun in sehr reduzierter Form. Sie nimmt nur den zentralen Teil des Schlosses ein, den sogenannten *corps de logis*. Wir wollen uns hier auf die wesentlichen Objekte und Kulturen konzentrieren. Diese „Essenz" des Sammlungsbestandes kommt dem Besucherwunsch entgegen, einen Überblick zu erhalten, der „verdaulich" klein, aber intensiv ist.

Format 2 sind semipermanente Ausstellungseinheiten. Davon wird es drei oder vier geben mit einer Größe von jeweils 160 qm. Sie werden jeweils im vorderen Teil des Westflügels eingerichtet. Wie der Name schon andeutet, werden diese Ausstellungen länger als eine Sonderausstellung, jedoch nicht fortwährend zu sehen sein (ca. 3–4 Jahre). Auch hier werden Objekte des Badischen Landesmuseums gezeigt, nun unter einer aktuellen thematischen Fragestellung: Sie präsentieren aktuelle Forschungsergebnisse, nehmen Jubiläen als Anlass, reagieren auf momentane politische oder gesellschaftliche Strömungen und Ereignisse oder fokussieren ein besonderes Objekt, bei dem viel Erklärungsbedarf besteht. Diese semipermanenten Ausstellungseinheiten sind uns sehr wichtig. Hier kann der Kurator sein eigentliches Können zeigen: die Interpretation des Objekts/der Objekte und ihrer gesellschaftlichen Relevanz.

Format 3 der Sammlungsausstellung wird das Schaudepot. Es wird sich über drei Stockwerke erstrecken und jeweils den westlichen Abschnitt jedes Stockwerks einnehmen. Das sind auf jedem Stockwerk ca. 400 qm, insgesamt zwei Drittel der Fläche des Westflügels. Weitere Flächen im zweiten Obergeschoss können noch dem Schaudepot zugeordnet werden.

Um das auf verschiedene Stockwerke verteilte Schaudepot als geschlossene Einheit zu begreifen und zu behandeln, ist ein Treppenhaus im hinteren Abschnitt des Westflügels notwendig, das teilweise schon vorhanden ist. Das Schaudepot soll in seiner Ausführung modern und hochwertig gestaltet werden, also nicht wie ein Arbeitsdepot. Trotzdem soll es eine große Menge von Objekten aufnehmen können. Die thematische Einrichtung erfolgt entsprechend der Zugehörigkeit der Sammlungsthemen auf demselben Stockwerk. So sind z.B. Objekte der Antike im Schaudepot im Erdgeschoss zu finden, die Schaudepot-Objekte des Spätmittelalters im ersten Obergeschoss usw. Innerhalb des Schaudepots wird es Zusammenstellungen von Objekten nach inhaltlichen Gesichtspunkten geben, nach kunst- und kulturgeschichtlichen Aspekten, aber auch reine Materialzusammenstellungen. Das eröffnet dem Besucher (als Einzelbesucher oder in einer Führung) das Angebot einer Vertiefungsebene.

Was ist nun neu an diesem Schaudepot? Schaudepots gibt es schon in anderen Museen, wie z.B. im Naturhistorischen Museum in Berlin oder im Vitra Museum in Weil am Rhein (Abb. 8). Drei Aspekte sind neu. In diesem Schaudepot gibt es zwar keine materiellen Objektschildchen, doch kann man virtuelle Informationen zu jedem einzelnen Objekt erhalten, denn die inhaltliche Erschließung der Exponate erfolgt digital. Der zweite Aspekt baut ebenfalls auf einer digitalen Erschließung auf: Man kann online durch sein Smartphone oder durch vor Ort befindliche „Endgeräte" (z.B. Tablets) Objekte sowohl aus der Expothek als auch aus dem Depot bestellen und sich vorlegen las-

Abb. 8 | Weil am Rhein, Vitra Museum, Schaudepot

sen. Zugrunde liegt die Idee, dass, ähnlich wie in einer Bibliothek, in der Bücher bestellt werden, nun Exponate durch den Nutzer bestellt werden können; daher nennen wir dieses Schaudepot entsprechend seiner Nutzung „Expothek".

Wie soll das Ganze nun funktionieren? Wie lange dauert so ein Bestellvorgang? Wenn ich etwas bestelle, kann ich das dann sofort sehen? Kann ich das Objekt auch anfassen? Gilt das Bestellprinzip für alle Objekte?

Prinzipiell soll es möglich sein, jedes Objekt zu bestellen, doch haben wir uns natürlich in Hinblick auf die Diversität der Objekte eine Lösung ausgedacht. Diese Lösung ist der dritte Aspekt und heißt „Oasen". Denn die Expothek ist ein Ort der intensiven Nutzung der Sammlung durch den Besucher bzw. Nutzer. Und genau dafür werden Raumeinheiten (Oasen) benötigt, die verschiedenartige Nutzungen ermöglichen. In einer „Oase" können dem Nutzer auf Wunsch Objekte vorgelegt werden, die ihm so unmittelbar nahe kommen, und im Idealfall kann er die Objekte im Wortsinn „begreifen". Um diesen Service zu organisieren, sollten die Nutzer die Objekte bereits vor ihrem Besuch online bestellen. Nach der Bestellung wird geprüft, bis zu welchem Grad die „Nahbarmachung" möglich ist.

Zusammengefasst: Kleinere Oasen werden an mehreren Stellen eingerichtet; auf Tischen werden die bestellten Objekte abgestellt und können auch angefasst werden, je nach Möglichkeit von Museumspersonen betreut.

Geht nicht? Doch, geht. Gibt es schon: *Yes, you can touch the object*. Hier zwei Beispiele: Ein Hands-on-Bereich in der historischen Library des British Museums (Abb. 9) und ein Science LAB im Historischen und Völkerkundlichen Museum in St. Gallen. Unbetreutes Anfassen halten wir für unnötig, denn der Mehrwert entsteht durch die Betreuung, das Gespräch. Es geht ja um die Wertigkeit des Objekts.

Für empfindliche Objekte wird eine „Studio-Oase" eingerichtet. Hier werden in einem geschützten und abgetrennten Raum die Objekte von einem Restaurator vorgelegt, und nur er übernimmt das *Handling* (Abb. 10). Den wissenschaftlichen Kollegen aus anderen Museen und Universitäten wird diese „Studio-Oase" ebenfalls zur Verfügung gestellt. Dort können Objekte gesammelt, vorbereitet und intensiv studiert werden.

Eine amphitheaterartig gestalte „Oase" (sogenanntes *Teatro anatomico*, Anatomiesaal in medizinischen Universitäten) ermöglicht Gruppen, um einen in der Mitte vorhandenen Tisch zu sitzen, z.B. um die Vorführung eines Objekts zu erleben (mit und ohne technische Hilfsmittel), um an spielerischem Wissensaustausch (z.B. einem Quiz) und an anderen Möglichkeiten

Abb. 9 | London, British Museum, Historische Bibliothek, Hands-on-Bereich

Abb. 10 | Restaurator mit Besucherin

objektbezogener Kommunikationsevents teilzunehmen.

Eine „Expo-Oase" besteht aus einer flexibel einzurichtenden Fläche und Vitrinen, mit der Nutzer – betreut vom Museumspersonal – kleine, zeitlich begrenzte Ausstellungen aus Objekten der Expothek selbst kreieren können. Diese Ausstellungsoase setzt die partizipative Idee der Expothek am deutlichsten um (Zielgruppen sind Studenten, Vereine, Interessensgruppen).

Nun soll es noch mehr „Oasen" geben, die nicht unmittelbar mit den Exponaten zu tun haben, aber die Expothek in einen belebten und angenehmen Ort verwandeln. So benötigen z.B. die Arbeit mit Sponsoren sowie bürgerliches Engagement eine „Oase" zum Versammeln, Kommunizieren und Beschließen. Diese „VIP-Oase" könnte im hinteren Raumabschnitt des Westflügels eingerichtet werden, mit der Möglichkeit, das Treppenhaus West des ersten Obergeschosses zu nutzen.

Eine „Biblio-Lounge-Oase" im ersten Obergeschoss im hinteren Teil des Westflügels lässt den Museumsbesucher in einem entspannten, wohnlich-behaglich und bibliotheksartig eingerichteten Raum Erholung finden. Publikationen zu aktuellen Ausstellungen sowie PC-Stationen mit dem digitalen Katalog der Sammlungen können bei einer Tasse Kaffee (Kaffee- und Kalt-Getränke-Automat) entspannt eingesehen werden. Der dortige Balkon ist ebenfalls begeh- und benutzbar. Ein Durchbruch der Decke zum zweiten Obergeschoss könnte dem Raum eine attraktive architektonische Note verleihen.

Abb. 11 | St. Gallen, Historisches Museum und Völkerkundemuseum, Science-LAB

Kleine „Oasen" sollten verteilt auf die drei Stockwerke ihren Platz finden, besonders Sitzgruppen ohne weitere Funktion (Silence-Oasen) oder mit Funktion, z.B. akustische Vermittlung mittels Kopfhörer oder PC-Stationen, bei denen der Besucher zu einem Beitrag aufgefordert wird, z.B. in einer „Lyric-Oase". Im Untergeschoss soll eine Art „All-Generations-Culture-Campus" entstehen. Kernstück wäre dann eine „Science-LAB-Oase", so wie z.B. in St. Gallen im Historischen und Völkerkundemuseum (Abb. 11).

Die Oasen-Idee soll keine Begrenzung finden. Es ist wichtig, dass moderne Anforderungen in das Konzept Eingang finden können. Manche Oasenidee muss im Laufe der Zeit „sterben" dürfen, dafür eine andere Oasenidee geboren werden können. So haben wir schon geplant, auch das Depotgebäude schrittweise zur Expothek auszubauen.

Abschließend ist festzuhalten, dass viele Ideen nicht neu sind, doch haben wir die für uns sinnvoll erscheinenden Ideen zusammengetragen und weiterentwickelt. Diese vielen Ideen der Nutzung und Vermittlung sollen keine kleinen Einzelaktionen bleiben, wie bisher andernorts gesehen, sondern hier als Gesamtkonzept konsequent durchgeführt werden. Das Herzstück des neuen Einrichtungskonzepts des Badischen Landesmuseums ist die digitale Strategie in Kombination mit der Expothek und ihren Oasen. Wir glauben, damit unser Museum gut in die Zukunft führen zu können.

Stockwerk	Westflügel	Westflügel vorn	Westliches Treppenhaus	Corps de logis	Westteil Zentraler Gebäudeteil	Ostflügel
2. OG	Expothek mit Treppe und Oasen	Semipermanente Ausstellung	Treppe Aufzug	1800 bis heute/ morgen	Funktionsräume	Oasen, Vorlegesaal
1.OG	Expothek mit Treppe und Oasen, Biblio-Lounge-Oase mit Balkon und Deckendurchbruch ins 2. OG	Semipermanente Ausstellung	Treppe Aufzug	13. Jh. bis 1800: Mittelalter, Kunst- und Wunderkammer, Renaissance, Waffenkammer, Türkenbeute, Barock, Landes- und Schlossgeschichte und Thronensemble	Frei zugänglich: „Baden-Heute"-Saal, Balkon und zentraler Saal	Sonderausstellung
Erdgeschoss	Expothek mit Treppe und Oasen	Semipermanente Ausstellung	Treppe Aufzug	Prolog und Antike:Prähistorie bis Byzanz, Völkerwanderung, Petershausener Portal (1173)	Foyer mit großem Aufzug	Sonderausstellung, Shop, Vortragssaal, Lastenaufzug, Personenaufzug
Keller	„All Generations Culture Campus"mit Science-LAB		Treppe Aufzug		Garderobe, Toiletten, Aufenthaltsraum	

Geplante Aufteilung des Badischen Landesmuseums Karlsruhe (Stand 2017)

Anmerkungen

1 Zur Verbesserung der Lesbarkeit wird im Folgenden überwiegend die männliche Version in der Bezeichnung von Personen verwendet. Im Sinne des Gleichbehandlungsgesetzes sind diese Bezeichnungen als nicht geschlechtsspezifisch zu betrachten. Sie sollen Frauen und Männer (oder: Personen aller Geschlechter) gleichsam einschließen.

2 Ernst Wagner: Über Museen und über die großherzoglichen Staatssammlungen für Altertums- und Völkerkunde in Karlsruhe. Vortrag, 4. Dez. 1904. Karlsruhe 1906, S. 3.

Literatur zur Sammlungsgeschichte des Badischen Landesmuseums (chronologisch geordnet):

Maaß, Michael: 150 Jahre Antikensammlungen in Karlsruhe 1838–1988. Karlsruhe 1988.

Grimm, Ulrike: Das Badische Landesmuseum in Karlsruhe. Zur Geschichte seiner Sammlungen. Karlsruhe 1993.

Hess, Regine (Hrsg.): Bauen und Zeigen – Aus Geschichte und Gegenwart der Kunsthalle Karlsruhe. Kat. Ausst. Bielefeld 2014.

Horst, Katarina: Antike in der Kunsthalle. In: Regine Hess (Hrsg.): Bauen und Zeigen – Aus Geschichte und Gegenwart der Kunsthalle Karlsruhe. Kat. Ausst. Bielefeld 2014, S. 114–123.

Uta Piereth

AM BEISPIEL: DIE NEUE DAUERAUSSTELLUNG „HERRSCHAFTZEITEN! ERLEBNIS CADOLZBURG" AB 2017

1. AUSGANGSLAGE

Cadolzburg – ein kleiner Ort mit einer großen Burganlage in der Nähe von Nürnberg. Nach dem Ende des Zweiten Weltkrieges lag die Anlage jahrzehntelang in ruinösem Zustand darnieder, seit den 1970er Jahren wurde sie mit starken Eingriffen baulich gesichert, verschiedene Nutzungskonzepte wurden durchgespielt, aber schlussendlich verworfen. In den 2000er Jahren machte man zumindest einen kleineren Teil der

Abb. 1 | Luftbild Cadolzburg

Burg auch innen für Veranstaltungen wieder zugänglich. Der größte Teil der Anlage war allerdings weiterhin ungenutzt und spiegelte verschiedene Ausbauzustände vom 13. bis ins 20. Jahrhundert wider (Abb. 1).

Ausgerechnet diese Cadolzburg sollte nun, wie 2012 von staatlicher Seite beschlossen, zu einem Burgerlebnismuseum werden? Die Konsequenzen dieser Entscheidung waren weitreichend: Der spätmittelalterliche Baukörper des Alten Schlosses musste auf zwei Etagen baulich erst wieder instand gesetzt werden. Weder ein Kassengebäude noch ein museales Nutzungskonzept waren vorhanden. Wie also war diese Aufgabenstellung aufzufassen – gerade angesichts der Tatsache, dass authentisch erhaltene Elemente des Mittelalters besonders im Inneren der Kernburg auf nur wenige Punkte beschränkt sind? Das Baudokument selbst konnte nur teilweise das Leben auf einer Burg im Mittelalter nachvollziehbar machen. Die Phase der Vernachlässigung und massive Kriegsschäden hatten außerdem dafür gesorgt, dass nahezu keine originalen Ausstattungselemente überliefert sind.

Der Bayerischen Schlösserverwaltung kam die Aufgabe zu, die Baumaßnahme zu betreuen und sich in einem zweiköpfigen Team seit 2013 auch den musealen Herausforderungen der Konzeptfindung und Realisierung eines neuen, dauerhaften Museumsbetriebs zu stellen.[1] Ziel sollte sein, die Burg gleichsam aus dem Dornröschenschlaf der Geschichte zu wecken und den Ort wieder neu im kulturellen Bewusstsein der Region und möglichst auch darüber hinaus zu verankern. Der Auftrag sah eine Belebung der Burg mit Mittelalterschwerpunkt vor, um ein möglichst breites Publikum und auch Familien ansprechen zu können.

2. KURZE BAU- UND NUTZERGESCHICHTE DES HAUSES

Ausgangs- und Angelpunkt war also der Bau selbst, dessen nachweisliche Anfänge in die Zeit um 1250 zurückreichen: Die Burggrafen von Nürnberg aus der Dynastie der (Hohen-) Zollern ließen sich hier einen stattlichen Herrschaftssitz bauen, von dem sich in der Kernburg die imposante Mantelmauer und Reste eines beachtlichen Palas sowie eines ersten, freistehenden Sakralbaus erhielten. Die ursprünglich schwäbischen Zollern hatten 1191/92 das Burggrafenamt im Dienste des Kaisers übernommen, doch dehnten die ehrgeizigen Herren ihren Aktionsradius rasch erfolgreich aus. Westlich und nördlich der ebenfalls aufstrebenden Stadt Nürnberg erwarben sie zahlreiche Ländereien und Rechtsansprüche. Dabei diente die Cadolzburg bald als Zentrum der wachsenden, ab 1363 sogar fürstengleichen Herrschaft. Der wichtigste Karrieresprung gelang den Zollern 1415/17, als sie mit der Kurwürde der Mark Brandenburg belehnt wurden, was einem enormen Machtzuwachs gleichkam, den sie im 15. Jahrhundert primär von Franken aus bewältigten (Abb. 2).

Die Bedeutungszunahme schlug sich auch in der Cadolzburg nieder: Das heute sogenannte Alte Schloss wurde repräsentativ, dem neuen Status angemessen ausgebaut, der Kapellentrakt aufgestockt und so eine Verbindung zum ehemaligen Palas geschaffen. Diesen älteren Baukörper baute man ab dem frühen 17. Jahrhundert ebenfalls zeitgemäß um, zum nunmehr „Neuen

Abb. 2 | Burgansicht von Westen: Blick auf Zwinger und Altes Schloss

Schloss". Solange die Hohenzollern in Franken regierten, nutzten sie die Cadolzburg dann als Nebenresidenz und Jagdschloss; in der Folgezeit diente die Burg bis ins 20. Jahrhundert als Amts- und Gerichtssitz. Im Kaiserreich erinnerten sich die Hohenzollern ihrer hier angesiedelten dynastischen Wurzeln durch herrschaftliche Besuche und Stiftungen; Burgenforscher dokumentierten den bis dahin unversehrten Burgbau. Um 1900 gab es eine erste museale Nutzung (für kirchliche Altertümer und als Burgmuseum); 1932 zog für kurze Zeit außerdem ein evangelisches Jugendferienheim ein, das unter den Nationalsozialisten durch die Einrichtung der HJ-Gebietsführerschule Josef Grün im Neuen Schloss ersetzt wurde. Wenige Tage vor Ende des Zweiten Weltkrieges ging am 17.4.1945 die Kernburg im Rahmen von massiven Schusswechseln zwischen den in der Burg verschanzten deutschen Resttruppen und amerikanischen Einheiten in Flammen auf. Die Burg blieb über Jahrzehnte als ungesicherte, gewaltige Ruine stehen – ein bedeutendes Kapitel fränkischer und deutscher Geschichte geriet so allgemein in Vergessenheit. Nach Beschluss des Wiederaufbaus im Jahr 1979 wurden zunächst massive Sicherungsmaßnahmen vorgenommen sowie die Dächer wieder gedeckt. Seit 2007 waren lediglich im Alten Schloss die zwei unteren Etagen baulich saniert und für Veranstaltungen regulär wieder zu nutzen.

3. METHODISCHE REFLEXIONEN IM VORFELD UND BEI DER KONZEPTIONELLEN UMSETZUNG

Angesichts dieser sozusagen zerklüfteten Geschichte war es den Kuratoren von vorneherein ein Anliegen, den Bau selbst zum primären Objekt der musealen Präsentation zu machen: Die Cadolzburg war als Denkmal ernst zu nehmen, die zahlreichen Brüche des Baukörpers sollten nicht mit dominanten Einbauten oder einer Inszenierung überdeckt werden. Zum andern galt es, über eine gewünschte alltägliche mittelalterliche Burgengeschichte hinaus die hochrangige Bedeutung der Burgherren in ihrer historischen, regionalen wie überregionalen Bedeutung zu profilieren und bewusst zu machen. Die Glanzzeit der zollerischen Fürsten aus Franken und auch die relativ gute Quellenlage zu den Hohenzollern im späten Mittelalter bildeten ein entscheidendes Kriterium für die Wahl des musealen Zeitschnitts: des 15. Jahrhunderts.

Sowohl die angestrebten architektonischen Lösungen (verantwortliches Architekturbüro: Claus + Forster, München) als auch die methodische Ausrichtung des Museums sollten den historischen Substanzverlust des Baukörpers und die Leerstellen in der (Re-) Konstruktion des Alltags im Spätmittelalter auf dieser Burg nicht überlagern, sondern in moderner Diktion thematisieren und kontextualisieren. Grundlegend war dabei die feste Überzeugung aller Projektbeteiligten, dass komplette Rekonstruktionen oder die Illusion von „vollständig wiederhergestelltem Mittelalter" auf keiner Ebene wirklich möglich und daher auch nicht erstrebenswert sind.[2] Vielmehr sollten die musealen Maßnahmen und Präsentationen Vorstellungshilfen geben, um sich auch auf der Objektbasis mit der gar nicht immer so fremden Vergangenheit auseinandersetzen und die eigene Wahrnehmung erweitern beziehungsweise schärfen zu können. Generell verfolgte das

Abb. 3 | Burgküche mit Ochsenschlot (hinter Glas)

Ausstellungs- und Vermittlungskonzept den Ansatz, Lust an selbstbestimmter, aktiver und teils auch gemeinschaftlicher Aneignung der Inhalte auf allen Ebenen bei den Besuchern zu fördern.[3]

Vor der Konkretisierung des inhaltlichen und methodischen Konzepts diente eine Befragung von Burgbesuchern und ein mehrmonatiges pädagogisches Projekt mit Grundschulkindern im Vorfeld der baubedingten Schließung dazu, für potentielle künftige Burgmuseumsbesucher interessante Themenfelder oder auch Nutzungsvorlieben zu sondieren. Einen Schritt weiter ging schließlich die Intention, möglichst vielfältige Einzelstationen in Kooperationen und mit partizipativen Ansätzen zu realisieren, um so spezifische regionale Kräfte und Perspektiven der zukünftigen Museumsnutzer aktiv in den Entstehungsprozess des Museums miteinzubeziehen.[4] Grundsätzlich wurden noch 2013 alle denkbaren methodischen und konzeptuellen Herangehensweisen zum Thema in einer deutschlandweiten Tagung mit einem breiten Kreis von Wissenschaftlern und Kuratoren unterschiedlichster Disziplinen diskutiert und reflektiert.[5]

Die Debatte über Zielgruppen des Museums wurde geführt, aber schlussendlich nicht zum Kernanliegen der Konzeption gemacht. Der ursprüngliche Auftrag umfasste zwar vorrangig Familien mit Kindern und Schulklassen als Zielpublikum, doch schien gerade die Profilierung als herausragende Dynastenburg und Brennpunkt deutscher Geschichte darüber hinaus ein primär geschichtlich interessiertes Publikum ansprechen zu können. Den konzeptionellen Überlegungen lag die Überzeugung zugrunde, dass komplexe Inhalte in verschiedenen Erschließungsformen auch für heterogene Besuchergruppen Potenziale und Zugänge bieten, ohne Beschränkung auf eine Altersklasse oder gar auf ein besonderes Deltamilieu.[6]

Solche Prämissen und Inhalte konkret in museale Realität zu übersetzen, hieß zunächst, den Besuchern weder ein verpflichtendes Lernpensum noch einen festgelegten Rundweg vorzugeben. Vielmehr galt es, ihr Interesse zu wecken, um selbständig Themen, Objekte und historische Verhältnisse zu entdecken. Gleichwohl wurden die historisch wichtigsten Inhalte – zu den Herren der Burg und zur Baugeschichte – so in die verschiedenen Rundgangmöglichkeiten integriert, dass sie stets von den Besuchern wahrgenommen werden. Die Themenzuordnungen ließen sich teilweise gut mit den baulichen Ausgangspunkten koordinieren und bringen so noch ablesbare Raumnutzungen zum Sprechen. Beispielsweise wird im Erdgeschoss das Thema Kochen und Ernährung dort präsentiert, wo sich tatsächlich ein gewaltiger Abzug über der Feuerstelle der ehemaligen Hofküche erhalten hat (Abb. 3). Auf diese Weise sorgt das Baudenkmal selbst für einen gewissermaßen niederschwelligen Einstieg in die Begegnung mit der Burggeschichte.

Abb. 4 | Augmented-Reality-Darstellung des Palas innen

Abb. 5 | Altes Schloss mit Ochsenschlot

Die Vielfalt an Präsentations- und Vermittlungsformen entspricht dem kuratorischen Credo: Originale Ausstellungsstücke werden in Vitrinen gezeigt und laden zur Begegnung mit der Dingwelt des späten Mittelalters ein. Eigens angefertigte, wissenschaftlich begleitete Reproduktionen verdeutlichen, wie aufwendig die Anfertigung hochrangiger Ausstattungsstücke (Kleidung, Rüstung, Wohnen) war. Interaktive und inszenierte Stationen ermöglichen schließlich das selbsttätige Ausprobieren und Verstehen bis hin zum freien Weiterentwickeln von Impulsen der angesprochenen Themen. Dabei ist nicht nur für Kopf und Hand etwas geboten, sondern auch für den Geruchs-, Geschmacks- und Gehörsinn – denn Geschichte vermittelt sich nicht nur über die Augen. Zeitgenössische mediale Vermittlungsformen sind fest in der Burg installiert und dort, wo es sinnvoll erscheint, um mobile Web-2.0-Anwendungsangebote ergänzt – so zum Beispiel im Bereich der Augmented Reality bei historischen Bauzuständen, die im jedermann zur Verfügung stehenden Multimediaguide abrufbar sind (Abb. 4).

Grundlage und Ausgangspunkt des musealen Vorgehens ist stets der enorme Fundus an aussagestarken Quellen zur Cadolzburg und zu den Hohenzollern im späten Mittelalter. Mit den Beiträgen im wissenschaftlichen Begleitband, der bereits im Vorlauf der Eröffnung vorlag,[7] und einem für die Ausstellung entwickelten Quellenmodul, den „Cadolzburger O-Tönen" in fest installierten Medienstationen,[8] sollte diese Basis auch dem Besucher offengelegt und zugänglich gemacht werden.[9]

Strukturell verankert sind außerdem zwei weitere Komponenten: zum einen ein Wechselausstellungsraum im Erdgeschoss, der mehrmals im Jahr Gelegenheit eröffnet, einzelne Facetten der Dauerausstellung gesondert zu vertiefen und so Anreize für erneute Burgbesuche zu bieten; zum anderen im obersten Museumsgeschoss ein großer Raum für Vermittlungsarbeit, in dem Workshops, Gesprächsrunden und Aktionen stattfinden können, die ebenfalls an die Ausstellung anknüpfen.

Von vorneherein mitgedacht und personell ermöglicht wurden außerdem vielfältige offene und buchbare Angebote für unterschiedlichste Zielgruppen und Interessen sowie ein anspruchsvolles, inhaltlich maßgeschneidertes Veranstaltungsprogramm.

4. DAS REALISIERTE MUSEUM

Aus den bisherigen Ausführungen ergibt sich, dass die Ausstellungsgestaltung kein Selbstzweck sein konnte, sondern im Rahmen eines komplexen Baudenkmals dieses selbst als primäres Exponat zur Geltung bringen sollte. Zugleich war eine große Bandbreite an Gestaltungskategorien zu beherrschen: klare Moderne im historischen Rahmen, gleichwohl die Fähigkeit, Vorstellungshilfen zu liefern, wo die originale Substanz defizitär ist, das Vermögen, spielerisch und metaphorisch Anreize zu schaffen, wo vermeintlich spröde Inhalte sonst abschrecken (jedoch ohne größere

Abb. 6 | Einführungsraum mit Narr Contz als Moderator, gezeichnet von Robert Kraus

Abb. 7 | Die Hohenzollern als Burgherren der Cadolzburg, Stammbauminszenierung und zwei Protagonisten

Abb. 8 | Baugeschichte in Modellen

inszenatorische Eingriffe), und die Bereitschaft, Medien dort einzusetzen, wo sie sinnvoll eine Ergänzung bieten können. Zugleich stellte die Größe der annähernd 2000 Quadratmeter Ausstellungsfläche allein im Alten Schloss eine logistische Herausforderung dar (Abb. 5).

Das renommierte und einschlägig ausgewiesene Büro Würth & Winderoll nahm sie an. Stilsicher und für Dauergebrauch robust in der Umsetzung realisierte das Büro das Projekt. Im Allgemeinen verliefen die Diskussionen im „magischen Dreieck" zwischen Kuratieren, Vermitteln und Gestalten konstruktiv, gelegentlich verteilte sich faktisch die Autoren-Rolle von Gestaltern und Kuratoren unterschiedlich.[10]

Die zugänglichen Teile der Burg und die museal angesprochenen Themen sowie deren Präsentationsformen, wie sie seit dem 24. Juni 2017 als Dauerausstellung eröffnet sind, sollen nun im Eilschritt kurz vorgestellt werden. Bereits in der großen, heute eher idyllischen und jederzeit zugängli-

Abb. 9 | Kapelle im zweiten Obergeschoss mit Bodenöffnung und Glasfenster der Jugendbauhütte Regensburg

Abb. 10 | Erkersaal mit angedeutetem Sterngewölbe

chen Vorburg beginnt das Burgerlebnis. An manchen Stellen lassen sich die Funktionszusammenhänge an den Kernburgbereich koppeln: Die Pferdeschwemme etwa erinnert an die Pflege der zeitweise zu Hunderten hier untergebrachten Pferde des fürstlichen Hofstaats; der Hungerturm diente als Gefängnis, die Haferscheune als Lagerort für Getreidevorräte, und der Garten ist durch seine Bepflanzung mit historischen Getreide- und Gemüsesorten ein Lern- und Erfahrungsort für Mittelalterkochkurse und Färbeworkshops. Mit Durchschreiten des inneren Burgtors beginnt der eigentliche museale Erzählzusammenhang. Es erklingen andere Töne, sowohl wörtlich als auch methodisch. Erste Hinweise laden ein zur Auseinandersetzung mit originalen Wehrelementen, Lichtnischen u.ä., ein riesiger Tretradkran sorgt für Aufsehen und die Möglichkeit, sich dem Thema des Burgbaus im Schatten der Mantelmauer nachvollziehbar zu nähern.[11] Im Innenhof hat der Besucher die Wahl, was er im Burginneren zuerst besichtigen will – gedruckte Übersichtspläne und fest installierte Etagenübersichten helfen dabei. Hat der Besucher bereits den großen Küchenschlot wahrgenommen, zieht es ihn meist zuerst ins Erdgeschoss. Hier erwarten ihn unter anderem der ruhige Brunnenhof (Thema: Wasserversorgung), der Einführungsraum mit dem unterhaltenden Comicfilm, in dem der archivalisch greifbare Narr Contz durch die wichtigsten Kapitel des Museums und der Zollernherrschaft führt (Abb. 6), sowie die Burgküche. Der Blick hinauf in den Abzug, Angebote für Nase, Gaumen, Augen, Hand und Hirn sowie für gelegentliche Selbstversuche (angelehnt an die historischen fürstlichen Rezepte) eröffnen hier gleich zu Beginn des Rundgangs viele Möglichkeiten des Burg-Erlebnisses à la Cadolzburg.

Im ersten Obergeschoss geht es um die zwei inhaltlich wichtigsten Facetten der Ausstellung: den Aufstieg der Zollern im späten Mittelalter und die Baugeschichte der Cadolzburg. Die Familie der Burgherren wird mit zwei Protagonistenpaaren – in teils aufwändigen materiellen und medialen Präsentationen – und einer dreidimensionalen, raumgreifenden Stammbauminszenierung vorgestellt (Abb. 7). Der Höhepunkt ihrer Karriere im Spätmittelalter wird mit der Schlüsselszene der Belehnung 1417 in einem Bild nachvollziehbar erzählt und das ambivalente Verhältnis der Burggrafen zur Stadt Nürnberg interaktiv zugänglich. Zwei Annexräume widmen sich einem sperrigen Thema (Macht und Recht) und einem sehr gefragten (Hygiene und Gesundheit), was jeweils an baugeschichtlich passenden Stellen – teils mit Augenzwinkern – aufgegriffen wird. Im zweiten Großraum der Etage konzentriert sich die Baugeschichte der Cadolzburg auf drei bauforscherisch erarbeitete Modelle (Abb. 8): ein Tischmodell der Kernburg um 1300, das Alte Schloss im Spätmittelalter in einem großen Modell, das in seinem Inneren Einblick gibt in das einstige Aussehen der bedeutenden Repräsentationsräume bzw. in die Konstruktion des Dachstuhls,[12] sowie der ruinöse Zustand beim Brand 1945 in einem Relief der Hoffront des Alten Schlosses. Einige Spiele, Infotafeln und Ansichten ergänzen diese kondensierte Darstellung.

Im zweiten Obergeschoss gelangt man in den wichtigsten Bereich der Burg zu Zeiten des Kurfürsten Albrecht Achilles. In der

Abb. 11 | Gut gerüstet: Harnischformen des Spätmittelalters zum Anprobieren

Abb. 12 | Fürstenbett und Dienerstrohsack zum Probeliegen in der „Kammer"

Kapelle ist die Gesamtanmutung und -ausstattung museal mit ansehnlichen fränkischen und brandenburgischen Kunstwerken; die Besonderheit als Doppel- (eigentlich sogar Dreifach-)Kapelle mit bauzeitlicher Bodenöffnung ist deutlich (Abb. 9).

Dagegen spricht in den beiden großen Repräsentationssälen stärker der Raumeindruck als die museale Inszenierung zum Besucher. Dies orientiert sich im Übrigen zugleich an den Nutzungsanforderungen, da in dieser Etage die Doppelfunktion als Museum und als Ort kultureller Veranstaltungen gewährleistet sein sollte. Während also außergewöhnliche architektonische und denkmalpflegerische Maßnahmen den Abglanz einstmaliger Prächtigkeit behutsam in ein gestalterisches Gesamtkonzept integrieren (Abb. 10), greifen Projektionen, Originale und Objekte zum Anfassen oder Ausprobieren sowie Medienstationen passgenau die Themen „Feste feiern im späten Mittelalter" und „Gotische Wölbkunst" auf.

Die umfassendste museale Ausstattung gibt es im dritten Obergeschoss. In den beiden Großräumen, die erst jüngst wiederhergestellt wurden und die architektonisch bewusst die heutige, nicht die Sprache des Mittelalters aufgreifen, werden ausführlich das Thema „Krieg im späten Mittelalter" sowie die Regierungs- und Verwaltungsstrukturen am Zollernhof in Franken und Brandenburg erörtert. Methodisch ist hier von Hands-On-Stationen über Spiele, über das Quellenmodul und hochwertige Reproduktionen bis hin zu kostbaren Originalobjekten des Spätmittelalters die gesamte

Bandbreite der auf der Cadolzburg eingesetzten Medien und Methoden zu erleben. Viele inhaltliche Facetten kommen dabei zum Tragen: nicht nur die Frage, wie die einzelnen Kämpfer speziell im späten Mittelalter gerüstet waren (Abb. 11), sondern auch, was Krieg damals ausgemacht hat – hinsichtlich technisch wie strategisch veränderter Formen der Kriegsführung und mit Blick auf die alltäglichen Probleme der einfachen Menschen unter steter Bedrohung durch die Kriegsgefahr.

Auch die „Alchemie" ist einer der an die Kriegsthematik anknüpfenden Aspekte auf der Cadolzburg. Sie erschöpfte sich nicht in esoterischen Bemühungen, denn sie brachte ebenso ganz handfest verwertbare naturwissenschaftliche Erkenntnisse für die Herren im montan- und pulverchemischen Bereich. Nachvollziehbare Versuchsanordnungen zeigen die Potenziale der damals wie heute genutzten Materialien. Ähnlich stellt sich „Regieren" durch Inszenierungen sowie spielerisch und medial übersetzte Ausstellungskomponenten als Summe von Einzelhandlungen, Strukturveränderungen und Kommunikationsverhalten dar – zu Zeiten, als es noch keine multimedialen Hilfsmittel gab. Der anstrengende Spagat zwischen unterschiedlichsten Territorien, Nöten und Ambitionen wird so erfahrbar. Auch der Hof war eine vielgliedrige Lebensform sowie eine Verwaltungsstruktur um den Herrscher herum, über den wir im Falle der fränkischen Zollern spannende Details kennen, die wir in anschauliche und aktivierende Stationen übertragen können – ob es nun den Stundenplan des Hofstaats,

Abb. 13 | Neues Schloss mit Medieninstallation

Abb. 14 | Turnierspaß und Reaktionsschnelligkeit, zu testen von Groß und Klein

Formen repräsentativer Unterhaltung oder standesbedingte Variationen des Schlafverhaltens angeht: Ein Strohsack einerseits und der Liegekomfort in einem Fürstenbett andererseits lassen sich beispielsweise testen, wodurch Ständegesellschaft unmittelbar fühlbar wird (Abb. 12).

Der Besucher verlässt das Museum meist über die imposante Freitreppe im dritten Obergeschoss, die vom Alten in das sogenannte Neue Schloss leitet. Dort dominiert der gewaltige Raumeindruck mit dicken Mauern, enormer Höhe (ohne Zwischendecken) und den Eingriffen im Dienste der Bausicherung, sprich: einem sichtbaren Betonskelett. Am Ende des Burgbesuchs steht damit ein besonders starker Eindruck und Kontrast zum bis dahin Erlebten und Gesehenen. Immer zur vollen Stunde füllt sich die heute riesige, nicht mehr unterteilte Raumhülle mit einer eigens für diesen Ort komponierten Klanginstallation des renommierten Klangkünstlers Gerald Fiebig. Er collagierte mit Melodien und Geräuschen eine Reise durch die bewegte 800-jährige Geschichte der Burg in 12 Minuten. Der Multimediaguide gewährt im Neuen Schloss nochmals einen Einblick in die Struktur des mittelalterlichen Palas, des ältesten Repräsentationsbaus der Burg, der im 16. Jahrhundert im späteren Renaissance-Baukörper aufging. Eine weitere museale Intervention widmet sich schließlich dem vorletzten Kapitel der Burgnutzung vor der aktuellen als Museum (Abb. 13): Im Rahmen eines pädagogischen Projekts des Dietrich-Bonhoeffer-Gymnasiums Oberasbach unter der Leitung von Felicitas

Handschuch haben Oberstufenschülerinnen und -schüler in Zeitzeugeninterviews nach Spuren der Nutzung der Cadolzburg als Hitlerjugend-Führerschule gesucht und nach dem verheerenden Brand 1945 gefragt. In Zusammenarbeit mit dem Künstler und Dramaturgen Pavel Franzusov wurde das Filmmaterial der Schüler für die Ausstellung in einer dreiteiligen Videoarbeit aufbereitet.[13]

5. DIE REZEPTION

Besucherzahlen sind nur eine Art, die Resonanz beim Publikum zu „messen". Im Falle der Cadolzburg darf man mit über 50 000 Besuchern in sechs Monaten bei einem musealen Neustart jenseits der Großstädte zufrieden sein. Viel mehr zählt jedoch, wie direkte persönliche Rückmeldungen von Besuchern, Beobachtungen in der Ausstellung, eine zwischen dem 19. Juli und 19. Oktober 2017 laufende Befragung sowie Notizen im Besucherbuch die Reaktionen derjenigen spiegeln, für die das Konzept erdacht und realisiert wurde. Ein insgesamt erfreulich positives Echo erreicht die Zuständigen von vielen Seiten, jüngst stand etwa im Besucherbuch „Die Burg schafft Begeisterung!" – was in der Kürze zahlreiche freundliche Äußerungen zusammenfasst und das Maximallob ist. Natürlich gibt es auch differenzierte Stimmen zu Einzelaspekten, beispielsweise „es war sehr schön, vor allen Dingen das Verwaltungsspiel. Das war toll und man musste gut zusammenarbeiten und sich sehr konzentrieren" oder aber Kritik über zuviel Raumklang im Hohenzollernraum und immer wieder nicht funktionierende technische Stationen. Tatsächlich ermöglicht der Medieneinsatz sowohl spielerische Anwendungen von Informationen und historischen Möglichkeiten als auch Visualisierung von Verlorenem. Aber selbst bei starkem Augenmerk auf „usability" in der Programmierung müssen auch elektrische Leitungen und Hardware robust funktionieren, und die Belastungen der Medienstationen sind durch dauernde Wartung zu parieren – eine stete Herausforderung für die Ausstellungspflege.

Generell herrscht im Museum – allemal wochenends – lebhafte Stimmung. Was an sich geschätzt wird von den Besuchern, nämlich der differenziert abzurufende Grad an Informationen, ist auf der Ebene konzentrierter Vertiefungen unter diesen Umständen mitunter eher anstrengend. Andererseits drückt sich in der belebten Atmosphäre gerade das aktive und kommunikative Entdecken der verschiedenen Angebote in der Burg durch kleinere Gruppen aus. Die Bandbreite der gewählten Methoden und Präsentationsformen erreicht offenbar tatsächlich ein großes Spektrum an Publikumsinteressen, und beileibe nicht nur diejenigen der Kinder (Abb.14).

Als mitreißend erweist sich die Burg insbesondere dort, wo die Themensetzung und der Bau selbst kongruent gehen, idealerweise kombiniert mit humorvollen oder überraschenden Komponenten. Anhaltend groß ist die Begeisterung über die Küche und den „neuen" Erkersaal, bemerkenswert die Ergriffenheit im Neuen Schloss angesichts des Raumes und der Videoarbeit, bei der die Verweildauer auch nach langen Burgbesuchen nochmals enorm hoch ist. Das Ausprobieren, das spielerische Aneignen und das Sinnliche werden von unterschiedlichsten Besuchern sehr geschätzt.

Erfreulich ist über dieses Faktum hinaus auch der in der Regel bislang pflegliche Umgang mit allen handhabbaren Museumselementen.

Die freie Wahl anzusteuernder Räume, Aspekte oder Zugänge kommt bei geschätzt 80–85 % der Besucher gut an, eine Minderheit beklagt, dass sie sich nicht genügend an die Hand genommen fühlt. Der ohne Aufpreis entleihbare Multimediaguide könnte hier Abhilfe schaffen mit der vorgeschlagenen Kurztour, doch entspricht das offenkundig nicht der Erwartung dieses Teils des Publikums. Im Übrigen verfügt der Medienguide über eine enorme Fülle an Zusatzinformationen, Expertenäußerungen, Bildern und Filmen, Sprachebenen und Augmented-Reality-Elementen; angesichts des reichen Angebots in der Dauerausstellung selbst nehmen die Besucher diese selten zusätzlich wahr. Überhaupt ist die „Klage" etlicher Besucher durchaus positiv zu bewerten, dass die museale Fülle und all das, was nach einem ersten Besuch noch zu entdecken bliebe, zu groß und folglich ein erneuter Besuch anzustreben sei: Von den befragten Besuchern gaben 79,7% an, nochmals wiederkommen zu wollen, was in Anbetracht der Lage Cadolzburgs immerhin bemerkenswert ist. Es scheint also, als sei dieser Kulturhunger nicht nach zwei Stunden gestillt.

Anmerkungen

1 Verantwortliche Kuratoren waren Dr. Uta Piereth und Dr. Sebastian Karnatz.

2 Vgl. die Tagung der Leibniz-Gemeinschaft in Mainz: Museen – Orte des Authentischen (März 2016) und den entsprechenden Beitrag von Karnatz/Pelludat/Piereth im (geplanten) Tagungsband.

3 Vgl. etwa Hans Belting: Das Museum als Medium. In: Ekkehard Mai (Hg.): Die Zukunft der Alten Meister. Perspektiven und Konzepte für das Kunstmuseum von heute. Köln/Weimar/Wien 2001, S. 31–43, bes. S. 41. 4 Vgl. dazu jüngst Anja Piontek: Museum und Partizipation. Theorie und Praxis kooperativer Ausstellungsprojekte und Beteiligungsangebote. Bielefeld 2017. – Dies verzahnte sich im Übrigen auch mit einem von vorneherein integrativ mitgedachten Marketingkonzept, da die Cadolzburg als bis dato weißer Fleck auf der kulturellen Landkarte breiter angelegte Unterstützung beim Start brauchte. Vgl. dazu: Hartmut John: Hülle mit Fülle. Museumskultur für alle – 2.0. In: Hartmut John / Anja Dauschek (Hgg.): Museen neu denken.

4 Perspektiven der Kulturvermittlung und Zielgruppenarbeit. Bielefeld 2008, S. 15–64, hier S. 21. – Anspruchsvolle partizipative Projekte liefen 2014–2017 tatsächlich über jeweils viele Monate, unter anderem mit verschiedenen schulischen Gruppen und mit den Jugendlichen des Freiwilligen Sozialen Jahres in der Denkmalpflege (Jugendbauhütte Regensburg). Deren ganz handfeste Ergebnisse wurden im Museum integriert, etwa in Gestalt eines Glasfensters in der Kapelle, des Zeitzeugenvideoprojektes im Neuen Schloss, des Stoffmusterbuches oder auch der Hörstationen „Burg im Ohr".

5 Wissen. Wahrnehmung. Vermittlung. Kulturgeschichte in der Öffentlichkeit. Tagung in München, 02./03.12.2013, mit zwei vorausgehenden Webtalks; veranstaltet von der Bayerischen Schlösserverwaltung und der Bundeszentrale für Politische Bildung. Publikation / URL: http://www.burg-cadolzburg.de/deutsch/service/catalog_3076572/index-sd.html#/1 (Stand: Mai 2018)

6 Deltamilieus liegen gewissermaßen quer zu den rein alters-, einkommens- oder geschlechtsbezogenen Sozialbetrachtungen und werden eher über kongruenten Lebensstil u.a. Kategorien gebildet, so die Ausführungen von Carsten Wippermann (vgl. z.B. ders.: Milieus in Bewegung. Werte, Sinn und Ästhetik in Deutschland. Würzburg 2011).

7 Unter Mitarbeit der diversen Spezialisten entstand das kurzgefasste wissenschaftliche Referenzwerk: Sebastian Karnatz / Uta Piereth (Hgg.): „herr im hauß". Die Cadolzburg als Herrschaftssitz der fränkischen Zollern im Mittelalter (= Forschungen zur Kunst- und Kulturgeschichte XII). München 2017. 2018 erscheint dann ein taschenbuchartiger Publikumsführer durch das fertige Haus.

8 Mit beispielhaften Originaltexten, deren Übertragung in Neuhochdeutsch und einer Audioversion.

9 Gleichwohl äußert sich in der Ausstellung kein abschließendes oder autoritativ vollständiges, behauptetes kuratorisches Wissen. Dies wird am Beispiel des offenen Umgangs mit dem Namensgeber der Cadolzburg deutlich: Von wissenschaftlicher Seite her ist keine eindeutige Fixierung eines bestimmten „Cadolt" möglich, der für die früheste Quellenerwähnung eines Zeugen „de Cadolzburg" 1157 verantwortlich zu machen wäre. Daher ist im Museum nach der Auflistung aller denkbaren Namensgeber die Möglichkeit gegeben, ein „Phantombild" zu zeichnen – und diesen als „Cadolt des Monats" auslosen zu lassen.

10 Vgl.: Heike Kirchhoff / Martin Schmidt (Hgg.): Das magische Dreieck. Die Museumsausstellung als Zusammenspiel von Kuratoren, Museumspädagogen und Gestaltern (= Schriften des Bundesverbands freiberuflicher Kulturwissenschaftler 1). Bielefeld 2007; sowie: Kai-Uwe Hemken (Hg.), Ute Famulla / Simon Großpietsch / Linda-Josephine Knop (Mitarbeit): Kritische Szenografie. Die Kunstausstellung im 21. Jahrhundert (= Image 64). Bielefeld 2015; sowie die Besprechung dazu von Anja Dorn, in: Journal für Kunstgeschichte 80 (2017) S. 460.

11 Bei Workshops kann er unter Aufsicht auch in Betrieb genommen werden.

12 Erarbeitet vom Lehrstuhl für Bauforschung der Technischen Universität München, Prof. Manfred Schuller.

13 Ein Impressum im 3. Obergeschoss des Alten Schlosses legt die Beteiligten am Projekt offen.

Literatur

Belting, Hans: Das Museum als Medium. In: Mai, Ekkehard (Hg.): Die Zukunft der Alten Meister. Perspektiven und Konzepte für das Kunstmuseum von heute. Köln/Weimar/Wien 2001.

Hemken, Kai-Uwe (Hg.) / Famulla, Ute / Großpietsch, Simon / Knop, Linda-Josephine (Mitarbeit): Kritische Szenografie. Die Kunstausstellung im 21. Jahrhundert (= Image 64). Bielefeld 2015.

John, Hartmut: Hülle mit Fülle. Museumskultur für alle – 2.0. In: John, Hartmut / Dauschek, Anja (Hgg.): Museen neu denken. Perspektiven der Kulturvermittlung und Zielgruppenarbeit. Bielefeld 2008.

Karnatz, Sebastian / Piereth, Uta (Hgg.): „herr im hauß". Die Cadolzburg als Herrschaftssitz der fränkischen Zollern im Mittelalter (= Forschungen zur Kunst- und Kulturgeschichte XII). München 2017.

Kirchhoff, Heike / Schmidt, Martin (Hgg.): Das magische Dreieck. Die Museumsausstellung als Zusammenspiel von Kuratoren, Museumspädagogen und Gestaltern (= Schriften des Bundesverbands freiberuflicher Kulturwissenschaftler 1). Bielefeld 2007.

Piontek, Anja: Museum und Partizipation. Theorie und Praxis kooperativer Ausstellungsprojekte und Beteiligungsangebote. Bielefeld 2017.

Wissen. Wahrnehmung. Vermittlung. Kulturgeschichte in der Öffentlichkeit. Tagung in München, 02./03.12.2013, mit zwei vorausgehenden Webtalks; veranstaltet von der Bayerischen Schlösserverwaltung und der Bundeszentrale für Politische Bildung. Publikation / URL: http://www.burg-cadolzburg.de/deutsch/service/catalog_3076572/index-sd.html#/1 (Stand: Mai 2018).

Abb. 15, Seite 76 | Thema Kleidung: Das „Mittelalter zum Überziehen", in einer spätgotischen Kleidertruhe präsentiert, wird ergänzt um ein blätterbares Stoffmusterbuch zu verschiedenen Textilien und Naturfarben

Abb. 16, Seite 77 | Thema Kommunikation: Die Inszenierung verdeutlicht mit zahlreichen Briefen, Zetteln und Boten das dichte Netz an Kommunikation mit den verschiedenen Herrschaftsgebieten der Zollern

Krappstrauch/Indischer Färberkrapp
(Rubia tinctorum/Rubia cordifolia)

Graue Eminenzen:
Fürstenberater und
Wege der Macht

Matthias Henkel

THE MUSEUM IS THE MESSAGE – AUSSTELLUNGSPRAXIS IM DIGITALEN ZEITALTER[1]

1. INTRO

„Ein Museum ist eine gemeinnützige, auf Dauer angelegte, der Öffentlichkeit zugängliche Einrichtung im Dienste der Gesellschaft und ihrer Entwicklung, die zum Zwecke des Studiums, der Bildung und des Erlebens materielle und immaterielle Zeugnisse von Menschen und ihrer Umwelt beschafft, bewahrt, erforscht, bekannt macht und ausstellt."[2] Der hier zitierte ICOM Code of Ethics spricht von „gemeinnützig", „auf Dauer angelegt", von „öffentlich" und „zugänglich", von „beschaffen, bewahren, erforschen, bekannt machen und ausstellen" – von Sonderausstellungen, die Ressourcen binden und Geld kosten, spricht er eigentlich nicht...

„Die Schausammlung des Museums, seine ständige Ausstellung, ist seine eigentliche Erscheinungsform. Die Geschichte der Museen lehrt, dass auch sie nicht völlig einfrieren, nicht permanent sein darf. Diesen Wechsel fordern die Museumsleute wie auch die interessierte Öffentlichkeit."[3] Auch dieses Zitat, der Denkschrift zur Lage der Museen in Deutschland von 1974 entnommen, spricht nicht von Sonderausstellungen – vielmehr von Schausammlungen, die dem Wandel zu unterwerfen seien.

Man könnte demnach von einem genetisch bedingten Strukturfehler des Museums sprechen: Eigentlich konzeptionell auf Dauer, ja auf Überdauern angelegt, ist das Museum heute zusehends und zugleich der Dynamik verpflichtet; dabei basiert die angestammte Personalstruktur vielerorts noch auf den Erfordernissen des vergangenen Jahrhunderts: Die eigentlich für die Kernkompetenz des Auf-Dauer-Ausstellens ausgebildete Belegschaft wird zur Produktion des Kurzzeitproduktes Sonderausstellung gewissermaßen missbraucht. Dieser Umstand wird deshalb tragisch, weil dadurch zugleich der Hege und Pflege der Schausammlung der personelle Boden entzogen wird. Erschwerend kommt hinzu, dass die museologische Halbwertzeit einer Dauerausstellung heute mit rund 10 Jahren angesetzt wird.

Das Museumswesen steht also zwischen Skylla – „Nichts ist so beständig wie der Wandel"[4] (= Sonderausstellungen) – und Charybdis – „Nichts ist so beständig wie ein Provisorium" (= Dauerausstellung). Zudem stehen wir vor einer technologisch-medialen Zeitenwende:

- Wir leben in einer Welt, in der das Gegenständliche immer mehr an Relevanz verliert. Heute finden Wertschöpfung und auch Arbeit mehr und mehr im Digitalen statt.
- Während ein Mensch etwa drei bis vier Tage ohne Wasser auskommt, tritt im Zeitalter der Smartphones der digitale Shutdown bei einem Stromausfall bereits nach circa 12 Stunden ein, nämlich dann, wenn der Akku leer ist.

Entwickelt sich also die Institution Museum in ihrer tradierten Form – als vornehmlich materielles Archiv – dieser Tage zu einem Paradoxon, zu einer unzeitgemäßen Einrichtung? Hat sich das Museum institutionell überlebt, oder besteht gerade in diesem Aus-der-Zeit-Gefallensein ein besonderer USP (Unique Selling Point) bzw. ein Alleinstellungsmerkmal?

Um zur Fragestellung, wohin sich die Institution Museum – und insbesondere das „Produkt Schausammlung" – zukünftig entwickeln könnte, tragfähige Überlegungen anstellen zu können, möchte ich im Sinne eines Parforce-Rittes zunächst skizzieren, woher die Institution Museum kommt. Diesen Überblick werde ich gleichzeitig für eine kursorische SWOT-Analyse im Hinblick auf den ICOM-Kanon nutzen.

2. MUSEOLOGISCHE PARADIGMEN

Die folgende Aufzählung ist nicht streng chronologisch zu verstehen, selbst wenn eine zeitliche Schichtung durchaus intendiert ist:

a. Die Wunderkammer – Das Objekt als Fetisch

In den Wunderkammern lag der Schwerpunkt in jedem Falle beim Präsentieren, wenn nicht sogar beim Re-Präsentieren. Schließlich waren die zumeist fürstlichen Sammlungen ein vorzeigbarer Bestandteil des jeweiligen Staatsschatzes.

Resümee: Museen sind von Beginn an symbolisch-politische Orte.

b. Entkontextualisierte Typologismen – Virchows Vitrinen

Durch die Auffächerung in einzelne Fachdisziplinen wuchs die Spezialisierungstiefe auch in den Museen. So wurden in der Archäologie chronologische Systeme erarbeitet, die stark auf der Analyse typologischer Entwicklungen basierten.

Resümee: Ordnung ist (nur) das halbe Leben: Die Systematisierung der Funde trägt zu größerer Ordnung bei, führt aber mitunter zur gedanklichen Entkontextualisierung.

c. Das Imaginäre Museum – André Malraux

Hätte André Malraux in den 1950er Jahren die digitalen Bildwelten des 21. Jahrhunderts vorausahnen können, er hätte seine helle Freude gehabt. Malraux nimmt einen Kulturvergleich vor, der wiederum auf typologischen und ikonographischen Erwägungen basiert.[5]

Resümee: Interkulturelle Vergleiche sind aufschlussreich, aber nicht unproblematisch.

d. Lernort contra Musentempel[6] – Herbert W. Kapitzki

Der Gipfelpunkt didaktisch ausgerichteter Expositorik war die Eröffnung des Historischen Museums Frankfurt/Main, „wo eine traditionsreiche Einrichtung neue edukativ reflektierte Ausstellungstechniken entwickelte."[7]

Resümee: Unzweifelhaft eine Zeit, in der die Museen das Vermitteln von Kontexten (durch Texte) in den Vordergrund stellten.[8]

e. Die Objektzentrierung, „Das Gold der Thraker"[9] und die Aura der Objekte – Walter Benjamin und Arne Eggebrecht

In den 1980er Jahren wurde ein Ausstellungstypus populär, der sich besonders auf die zur Schau gestellte Aura der Objekte verließ. In einer dem Juwelierhandel entlehnten Szenographie wurden Gegenstände – vornehmlich aus Edelmetall – dem im Halbdunkel in Schlange stehenden, staunenden Publikum präsentiert.

Resümee: Die Bedeutung von Licht und Schatten für eine gezielte Blickführung ist spätestens mit Rembrandts innovativer Malweise im Kunst- und Kultursektor bekannt, verfehlt aber auch heute nicht ihre fokussierende Wirkung.

f. „Preußen. Versuch einer Bilanz" – Gottfried Korff

Kulturhistorische Großausstellungen zogen seinerzeit viele Besucher an, deren Konzeption auch als „objektgestützte Themenorientierung" bezeichnet werden kann.[10] Damit war das Format der Blockbuster-Ausstellung geboren und somit das Wohl und Wehe des Museumswesens.[11]

g. Rekontextualisierung – oder: Wilhelm von Bodes „Period Rooms" und die Freilichtmuseen

In diesem Zusammenhang plädiert Könenkamp 1988 in seinem noch heute lesenswerten Artikel für die bedeutungsvolle Zurschaustellung der Exponate.[12]

Resümee: Schon Wilhelm von Bode hat mit seinen Period Rooms im 1904 eröffneten Kaiser-Friedrich-Museum (heute: Bode-Museum) eine ähnliche Strategie verfolgt, der noch heute viele Freilichtmuseen anhängen.

h. Das Sentimentale Museum – Daniel Spoerri

Früh beschritt Daniel Spoerri mit seinem Konzept des „Sentimentalen Museums" einen ganz besonderen, emotionalen Weg.[13]

Resümee: Man könnte diesen subjektiven Ansatz des Exponierens in der Rückschau als einen konzeptionellen Vorläufer der heute geläufiger werdenden Ausstellungspraxis der Partizipation / Co-Produktion verstehen.[14]

i. Die Identitätsfabrik – Gottfried Korff und Martin Roth

Mit dieser Publikation von 1990 gelang es Korff/Roth, das diversifizierte Spektrum des Museumswesens jener Zeit auszuleuchten.[15]

j. Expo 2000[16] – Das Primat des inszenierten Raumes – Martin Roth

Mit der Expo 2000 wurde das Thema Szenographie im Museum virulent.

Resümee: Die Ausstellungsbereiche in der EXPO 2000 wurden als Themenparks – als Erlebnislandschaften – gestaltet. Vergleichbare Gestaltungsprinzipien werden heute in Brand Centers von Markenartiklern rezipiert, bei denen das möglichst sinnliche, intuitive Markenerlebnis im Fokus des Vermittlungs- und Verkaufsinteresses steht.[17]

k. Das Analoge und das Digitale[18]

Nach der ersten Welle des Einzugs schwerfälliger PC-Technologie in das Ausstellungswesen, das häufig mit dem Schild *„Leider derzeit außer Betrieb!"* gekennzeichnet war, hat sich das Digitale zwischenzeitlich im Museums- und Ausstellungswesen fest etabliert.

Resümee: Insbesondere der Faszination des Bewegtbildes können sich auch die AusstellungsbesucherInnen nicht entziehen. Der didaktisch-pädagogische Streit ist damit vorprogrammiert, ob denn das Digitale das Analoge stützt oder im Gegenteil gar verdrängt.

l. Das Virtuelle Museum[19]

Die mögliche Konsequenz einer stringent fortgesetzten Medialisierung des Museums hätte im Virtuellen Museum münden können. Wie schnell jedoch technologische und gestalterische Entwürfe im rein Medialen veralten, lässt sich am Beispiel des Virtual Museum of Canada – „…The largest digital source of stories and experiences shared by Canada's museums and heritage organizations" – sehr eindrucksvoll veranschaulichen.[20]

m. Das Partizipative Museum[21] und Audience Development

Mit dem Web 2.0 und auch in der Folge der New Museology hat sich das Thema der Partizipation und der Co-Produktion im Museum zu einem echten Megatrend entwickelt.[22]

Resümee: Während das *Museum als Lernort* bei allen kulturpolitischen Redenschreibern inzwischen geläufig ist, sind partizipative Praktiken im deutschen Sprachraum zwar viel diskutiert, jedoch noch nicht fest institutionell verankert. Konsequent fortentwickelt, würde schließlich die Institution Museum einen großen Teil ihrer Deutungskompetenz in Frage stellen. In jedem Falle aber würde es der Fortbildung des angestammten Personals bedürfen, um offene Dialoge und diskursive Interaktionen mit den partizipierenden und co-produzierenden BesucherInnen überhaupt moderieren zu können. Auch die ganzheitlichen Strategien des Audience Development mit ihrer konsequent auf den Besucher ausgerichteten Perspektive stellen eine besondere Herausforderung für das angestammte Museumspersonal dar.[23]

n. Big Data, Web, Social Media, Open Source[24]

Datentechnisch betrachtet, handelt es sich bei Museen gewissermaßen um Massenspeicher heterogener, nicht kompatibler, lückenhafter Datenbestände. Dies ist weit entfernt von dem, was im heutigen Wortgebrauch unter Big Data verstanden wird.[25]

Resümee: Wie können wir die vorhandenen Daten so erschließen, dass sie gesellschaftlich nützlich anwendbar und verwertbar sind? Immerhin könnten die Museen dadurch in der zu führenden Relevanz-Debatte deutlich an Boden gewinnen.

o. Das Museum als moralisch-ethische Herausforderung – Emanuel Macron[26]

Am 28. November 2017 umriss der französische Staatspräsident Emmanuel Macron in einer Grundsatzrede an der Universität Ouagadougou in Burkina Faso die Herausforderungen, vor denen Afrika, Frankreich und Europa in ihren Beziehungen stehen. Zur Frage der Restitution afrikanischen Kulturgutes machte er folgende

Aussage: „Ich möchte, dass innerhalb der nächsten fünf Jahre die Voraussetzungen für zeitweilige oder endgültige Restitutionen des afrikanisches Erbes an Afrika geschaffen werden." Auf Twitter legt der Elysée-Palast nach: „Das afrikanische Erbe darf kein Gefangener europäischer Museen sein."[27] Die kulturpolitischen Auswirkungen dieser von Macron getroffenen Aussage sind zum jetzigen Zeitpunkt in ihrer Tragweite noch nicht abzusehen. Zu verstehen sind diese Worte vor dem Hintergrund der sogenannten Washingtoner Prinzipien,[28] des „Schwabinger Kunstfundes"[29] und der damit zusammenhängenden Debatte um den Umgang mit NS-verfolgungsbedingtem Kunst- und Kulturgutverbleib. Kann die Notwendigkeit zur Erforschung der Provenienz für NS-verfolgungsbedingten Entzug von Gütern inzwischen als allgemein unbestritten angesehen werden, wird – befeuert auch durch das im Bau befindliche Humboldt-Forum – die öffentliche Debatte um den entsprechenden Umgang mit ethnologischen bzw. archäologischen Sammlungsbeständen erst seit kurzem geführt. Ohne das Ergebnis dieser laufenden Diskussion vorwegnehmen zu wollen, ist eines evident: Damit die Institution Museum auch weiterhin ihre auf Fakten und Artefakten basierende dokumentarische Reputation behalten kann, bedarf es künftig eines deutlich höheren Maßes an Transparenz in Bezug auf die öffentliche Zugänglichkeit der Quellenlage zur Provenienz.

Zwischenresümee

Dieser kurze Blick auf die Entwicklung der Institution Museum macht deutlich: Museen sind Experten des Sich-Wandelns. Die Entwicklung basiert jeweils auf einer Schwerpunktverlagerung innerhalb der museologischen Matrix zwischen Sammeln, Bewahren, Erforschen, Präsentieren und Vermitteln, die zunehmend auch durch neue Handlungsfelder (Inszenieren, Kommunizieren, Partizipieren) anzureichern sein wird.

Dennoch – oder gerade deshalb – besitzen Museen die Fähigkeit, auch künftig zentrale Orte gesellschaftlicher Bewusstseinsbildung zu sein. Dass daran Bedarf besteht, ist – im Zeitalter der Ausdünnung der politischen Mitte – mehr als offensichtlich.[30]

3. THE MUSEUM IS THE MESSAGE

Mit Absicht bezieht sich diese Zwischenüberschrift auf das Werk von Marshall McLuhan.[31] Museen sind heute im wahrsten Sinne des Wortes zu Massenmedien geworden. Es ist daher sinnvoll, bei Überlegungen zur zukünftigen Bedeutung der Institution Museum insbesondere die Wirkungsweise und Wirksamkeit, die möglichen Potenziale und auch die institutionellen Grenzen in den Blick zu nehmen. Eine der elementaren Herausforderungen formuliert die Direktorin der Tate, Frances Morris, in einem Interview folgendermaßen: „Wer weiß, vielleicht ist die nächste Herausforderung der virtuelle Raum? Dann brauchen wir gar keine Galerie mehr. Das ist die große Frage: Wie geht es nach der Post-Galerie weiter?"[32] Welche Strategien können Museen also für ihre Schausammlungen entwickeln, um auf diese Zeitenwende produktiv zu reagieren?

Das nicht nur kommunikative Instrumentarium für eine Fortentwicklung der Institution Museum ist mehr als reichhaltig. Auch hier geht es daher im Folgenden eher um einen spannungsreichen Einblick und nicht um einen vollständigen Überblick:

Digitalisierung der Bestände

Das Web wird von den Museen bislang eher konventionell als zusätzliches Medium zur ausstellungsbegleitenden Kommunikation genutzt. Noch ist es m.E. nicht gelungen, diesen physikalisch unbegrenzten Raum wirklich authentisch zu nutzen – d.h. wirklich zu kuratieren.[33] Demgegenüber sind die sich inzwischen durchsetzenden Bemühungen zur Digitalisierung von Sammlungsbeständen als positiv zu bewerten.[34]

Soziale Medien

Twitter, Facebook, Instagram und Co. gehören inzwischen mehr oder minder zum Instrumentarium der Kommunikationsabteilungen in Museen; auch hier allerdings, ohne dass bislang ein eigenständig-authentischer Kommunikationsstil entwickelt worden wäre. Wie produktiv der Umgang mit historischem Quellenmaterial im Bereich der Sozialen Medien sein kann, hat hingegen die Stiftung Brandenburger Tor mit der Ausstellung über Harry Graf Kessler unter Beweis stellen können.[35] Auch der seit 2010 auf Twitter kommunizierte AskACurator-Day hat sich zu einer festen Größe entwickelt.[36]

Ganz allgemein ist der Einsatz der Sozialen Medien weniger wegen des direkten finanziellen Aufwands problematisch, sondern vielmehr durch die hohe Personalkapazität, die dadurch langfristig gebunden wird. Auch die hohe Kommunikationsfrequenz, die nicht den angestammten musealen Kommunikationsgewohnheiten entspricht, vereitelt mitunter, dass die Aktivitäten in diesem Feld auf einem wirklich strategisch ausgearbeiteten, markenbildenden Konzept beruhen.

Virtuelle Rundgänge

Mit einem hohen technischen Aufwand wird das GoogleArtProject betrieben.[37] Die feinsinnige Rezension von Beat Wyss macht jedoch deutlich, dass der im Netz entstandene Reinraum nicht leicht zu bespielen ist, das Museumsgefühl mithin abhandenkommt.[38]

Virtuelle Ausstellungen

Inzwischen gibt es Plattformen wie Kunstmatrix, die es jedermann ermöglichen, eine Online-Ausstellung zu kuratieren. Der septisch wirkende Ausstellungsraum bietet jedoch nur wenig Aufenthaltsqualität.[39] Das im Entstehen befindliche virtuelle Migrationsmuseum wirkt – zumindest im Trailer – dagegen professioneller.[40] Eine durchaus beeindruckende Anwendung hat die Firma Adidas für ihr Firmenarchiv entwickelt: eine gelungene Mischung aus Objektpräsentation und Kontext, die durch das Storytelling-Element einen echten Zusatznutzen bietet.[41]

Museumsführung 2.0

Eine unkonventionelle Fortentwicklung der klassischen Führung bietet Museum Hack.[42] Mit dem Slogan „This Isn't Your Grandma's Museum Tour" wird deutlich, dass das Hauptinteresse des Anbieters darin liegt, den Besuchern einen erlebnisorientierten Weg durch das Museum zu bieten.

Auf dem Weg zur (Web)App – BYOD[43] statt Multimediaguides[44]

Das Zeitalter des klassischen Audioguide geht zu Ende. Dazu gesellt sich auch der im Museum vorgehaltene Multimediaguide. Getreu der Devise *Bring your own Device* wird bei der individuellen, multimedialen Vermittlung im Museum künftig das Endgerät des Besuchers direkt zum Einsatz kommen.[45] Die Argumente für eine solche Entwicklung sind schlagend: Die Kosten für Anschaffung und Wartung der Geräte werden an den Besucher ausgelagert. Außerdem sind die Besucher mit der Handhabung ihrer eigenen Geräte vertraut. Entscheidend bei der Durchsetzung dieser Technologie ist allerdings die abschließende Klärung der rechtlichen Frage nach einem freien WLAN-Zugang.[46] Denn sonst wird es für Touristen – und das sind nun mal die Mehrzahl der BesucherInnen – im Noch-Zeitalter von Roaming-Gebühren teuer.[47]

Video / Bewegtbild

Das Medium Bewegtbild ist aus unserer Alltagskommunikation nicht mehr wegzudenken: Wer heute ein Rezept sucht, schaut nicht mehr in Omas Kochbuch, sondern bei YouTube, wie das Steak oder der Grünkernbratling am besten gelingt.

Das British Museum hat einen YouTube-Kanal unter dem Titel „Curator's Corner".[48] Die in diesem Format gezeigten Filme sind allerdings mit 5–7 Minuten für aktuelle Sehgewohnheiten relativ lang. Das Rijksmuseum in Amsterdam setzt hingegen auf sehr kurze Clips. Diese sind auch mobil gut zu konsumieren.[49] Auch themenzentrierte Ausstellungen werden auf diese Weise professionell beworben.[50]

Mit seinem Welcome-Video zeigt das Rijksmuseum konsequent, wie Besucherorientierung wirklich funktioniert: Nicht die Exponate sind im Film zu sehen, sondern deren Wirkung auf die Besucher: staunende, vertiefte, interessierte Menschen jeden Alters, jeden Geschlechts oder jeder Weltanschauung stehen im Fokus. In nicht einmal 2 Minuten wird echte Sehn-Sucht erzeugt: Audience Development at its best.[51]

Im deutschsprachigen Raum ist das Städel Museum unter seinem inzwischen nach New York gewechselten Direktor Max Hollein im Medien-Bereich ausgesprochen aktiv gewesen. Der Städel-YouTube-Kanal verzeichnet derzeit rund 170 Clips. Tendenziell sind hier die Filme deutlich länger als beim Rijksmuseum Amsterdam. Die deutlich niedrigere Zahl von Aufrufen zeigt, dass damit wohl auch der Publikumsgeschmack nicht voll getroffen wird.[52]

Merchandising – customized

Das Thema Merchandising ist im deutschsprachigen Raum bislang ausgesprochen unterentwickelt, vergleicht man es mit den Verhältnissen in den USA oder China. Dies nicht zuletzt deshalb, weil für hochwertige Produkte auch hohe Anlaufkosten für die Entwicklung und Produktion vorfinanziert werden müssen und die öffentlich geförderten Einrichtungen solche strategischen Investitionen mitunter schlecht verbuchen können. Langfristig zahlt sich jedoch eine solche Investition aus, wenn damit zugleich die eigene Marke emotional aufgeladen und zusätzlich gestärkt werden kann. Das Rijksmuseum Amsterdam setzt auch hier ganz auf die Kreativität seiner Besucher: Mit Hilfe des Rijksstudio kann sich jeder Besucher sein eigenes Merchandising-Produkt selbst gestalten – ein kurzer Video-Clip erklärt, wie es funktioniert.[53]

Blog

Der privat betriebene Blog Kultur-Museum-Talk verzeichnet derzeit im deutschsprachigen Raum rund 95 aktive Museumsblogs.[54] Eine niederländische Website führt die 100 besten Museums- und Kuratoren-Blogs aus dem englischsprachigen Raum auf.[55] Auch das Städel Museum ist mit einem sehr hochwertigen Blog seit 2011 im Netz vertreten.[56] Wenn man die Anzahl an Kommentaren als indirektes Indiz für Nutzungshäufigkeit nimmt, wird das Format des Blog allerdings eher verhalten genutzt.

Immersivität und Augmented Reality (AR)

Beide Themen werden, da die technisch bedingten Produktionskosten derzeit noch rapide sinken, erst in Zukunft im Museumsbetrieb eine größere Rolle spielen. Hingegen sind diese Technologien im Spielesektor seit Jahren fest verankert. Aber auch im Bereich der Archäologie wird schon länger mit Augmented Reality-Methoden gearbeitet, um Rekonstruktionen möglichst wirklichkeitsgetreu visualisieren zu können. Einen allerdings nur kurzfristig wirksamen Popularisierungsschub hat das Thema AR durch den Launch von Pokémon Go im Sommer 2016 erhalten.[57]

4. SOME KEYWORDS FOR THE MUSEUM AS A MESSENGER

Wenn das Museum heute als eine Botschaft, als ein multimedialer Newsroom[58] zu verstehen ist, dann gilt es hier, das zeitgenössische und zugleich authentische Instrumentarium zu definieren, mit dem sich das Museum am gesellschaftlichen Diskurs produktiv beteiligen kann.

content-related (materiell / immateriell)

Der Blick in die institutionelle Geschichte des Museums hat gezeigt: Das absolute Alleinstellungsmerkmal des Museums besteht in seiner materiellen Content-Kompetenz. Um zukunftssicher zu werden, sollte das Museum darüber hinaus aber auch die Kompetenzen für das Immaterielle, das Digitale und das Virtuelle erwerben.[59]

Die plakative Wahrheit des Content-Marketing lässt sich in drei Kategorien fassen, die von der Wahrnehmung des Kunden bzw. des Publikums ausgehen:

- ein Zuviel an Information vermeiden,
- keine Zeit verschwenden,
- liefern, was gebraucht wird.[60]

Der letztgenannte Aspekt sollte in Bezug auf das Museum nicht subjektiv, sondern gesellschaftlich – d.h. aus der Perspektive der potentiellen Besucher – betrachtet werden. Jürgen Habermas hat bereits 1985 von der „Neuen Unübersichtlichkeit" gesprochen. Doch: Wie viel unübersichtlicher ist die Welt seitdem geworden?[61] Es besteht für die Museen eine große Chance darin, den Besuchern insbesondere Orientierungswissen zu vermitteln, um damit ein eigenständiges Weiterdenken außerhalb des Museums zu ermöglichen. Alle diesbezüglichen Überlegungen haben einen ganzheitlichen Einfluss auf die Art und Weise, wie wir künftig Museum denken. Das bedeutet, die Revolution der Kontextinformation fängt beim Klingelschild an und hört bei der Kuratierung der Objektbeschriftung noch nicht auf (Visitor Journey).

communicative

Da die Leitmedien (Presse, Funk, Fernsehen, Web) heute stark empörungsgetrieben berichterstatten, muss das Museum als Newsroom auch selbst zum Sender seiner eigenen Botschaften werden, sonst wird die Vermittlung der zum Teil komplexen Inhalte unter der andauernden Verkürzung leiden. Insbesondere die Kommunikationsstrategien zu Schausammlungen müssen fortentwickelt werden, um Stärken zu profilieren, um Berichtsanlässe zu schaffen und um polyperspektivische Zugänge zu ermöglichen. Dazu gehört es auch, Botschafter – neudeutsch: Influencer – für die Institution Museum zu gewinnen.[62]

responsive (im Sinne von besucherorientiert)

Über lange Zeiten hinweg war das Museum mehr oder weniger ausschließlich als *Sender* aktiv. Um Besucher und insbesondere Nicht-Besucher ansprechen zu können, ist jedoch eine Bereitschaft zur institutionellen Öffnung erforderlich. Guter Wille ist da erst nur die Basis. Zusätzlich bedarf es des Erwerbs neuer, sozialer Kompetenzen auf der Seite der Museumsbelegschaft. Die damit verbundene Perspektive für die Institution Museum, so die Voraussetzungen zu schaffen, sich zu einem „Third Place" im Sinne von Ray Oldenburg zu entwickeln, sollte jedoch verlockend sein[63] – benötigen unsere modernen Gesellschaften doch dringend angstfreie, soziale Räume, um miteinander den Diskurs über unterschiedliche Wertvorstellungen führen zu können. Überaus spannend in diesem Zusammenhang ist das von Ram Adhar Mall entwickelte Konzept der kulturellen Überlappungen, einer „Hermeneutik jenseits der Identität und Differenz."[64]

relevant (lebensnah / mit einem Bezug zur Lebenswelt unserer BesucherInnen)

Die Museen werden dann ihr Publikum auch weiterhin erreichen, wenn sie Produkte anbieten, die die Kundschaft interessieren.[65] Dies ist dann der Fall, wenn das Interesse geweckt werden kann für das Außergewöhnliche, für das Unbekannte, für das Eigene, für das Andere – vor allem aber für das, was einen selbst betrifft. Alltagsrelevanz von Ausstellungsthemen (auch in der Schausammlung) kann dann gelingen, wenn für die Besu-

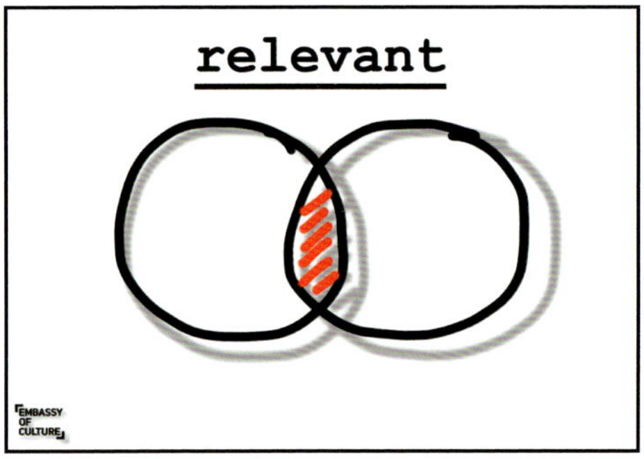

cherInnen ein Gegenwartsbezug erkennbar wird.[66]

interconnected (über alle Informationsebenen hinweg verknüpft)

Interkonnektivität heißt, Zugänge zu schaffen, um Informationen von unterschiedlichen Ebenen miteinander in Beziehung zu setzen, ohne dass es zu einer Depression angesichts der ansteigenden Komplexität der Themen kommt. Und: Es geht um eine auch medial gestützte Ausweitung des Museums über seine angestammten räumlichen und spartenbezogenen Grenzen hinweg. Dazu gehört auch die Vermeidung von Medienbrüchen: Wie bei einer guten Wegeleitung darf der Kontakt zum Kunden (vulgo: BesucherIn) nicht abbrechen. Das Museum der Zukunft sollte daher auf allen Kanälen ansprechbar sein: 24/7/365.

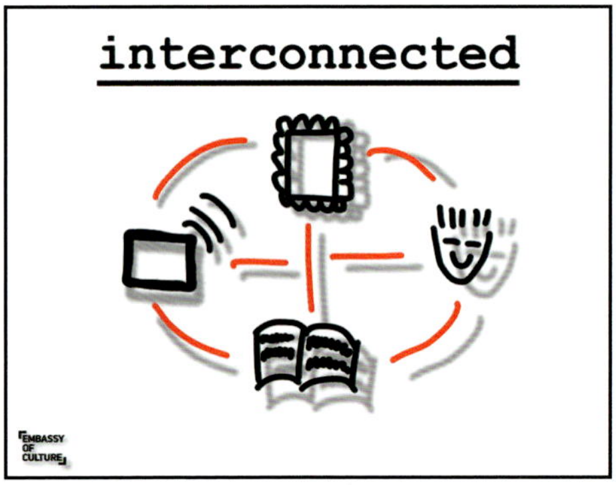

transmedial (medienübergreifend)

Wir leben am Beginn einer durch und durch medialisierenden Epoche. Es liegt daher nahe, das Museum auch als medienübergreifendes Massenmedium zu verstehen. Das bedeutet nicht, dass das Objekt vor lauter Bildschirmen nicht mehr erkennbar sein sollte. Aber es bedeutet, für die nötigen Informationen die jeweils authentischen Medienkanäle und Formate zu nutzen. Für das Museum ist das World Wide Web bislang vornehmlich Kommunikationsmedium. Es sollte aber gelingen, es künftig als Quelle und schließlich als ein *additional space for exhibitions* zu erschließen und authentisch zu kuratieren.[67]

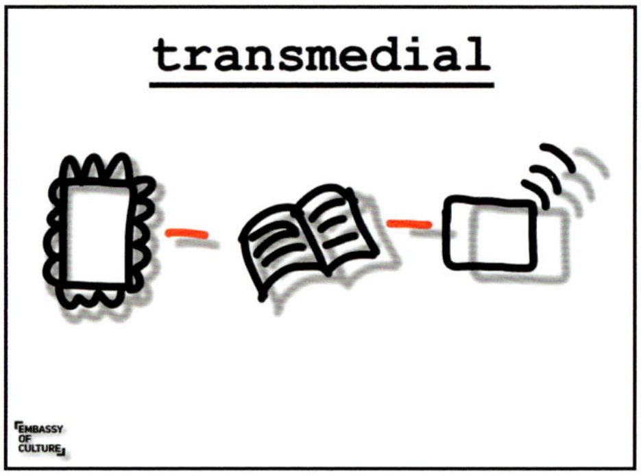

emotional (berührend, erzählend)

Das Museum hat über weite Strecken seiner institutionellen Geschichte glaubhaft versichert, neutral, ja objektiv zu sein, nur darzustellen. Ausstellungen, auch Schausammlungen sind aber zugleich auch Inszenierungen, d.h. Interpretationen. Wenn die Museen künftig dafür sorgen, dass das Faktische und das Hypothetische für den Besucher erkennbar bleibt, könnten sie ruhig öfter einen *Emotional Approach* wagen.

Durch partizipative Konzepte oder gar coproduzierte Projekte wird über kurz oder lang ohnehin der subjektive Blick deutlich stärker im Museum Raum greifen. Entscheidend ist die Kennzeichnungspflicht – ähnlich wie bei den Zusatzstoffen in der Wurst- und Käsetheke. Letztendlich befassen sich Museen seit fünf Jahrhunderten mit dem Erzählen von Geschichte(n). Es besteht also eigentlich eine lange Erfahrung im Storytelling.

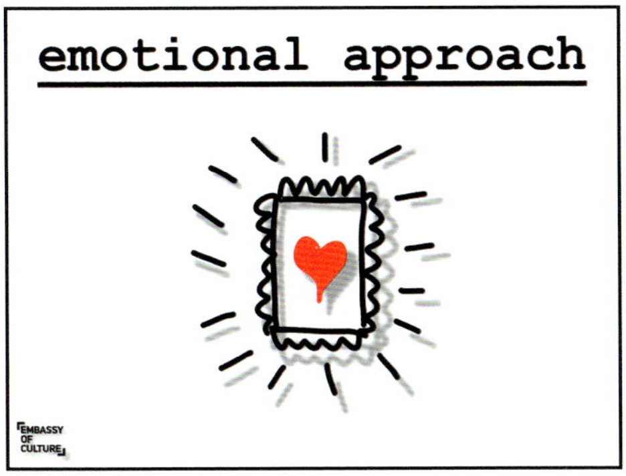

visual design[68] (Szenographie)

Das, was in den Sonderausstellungen schon gang und gäbe ist, sollte vermehrt auch in die Schausammlungen einziehen: die pointierte Gestaltung der Räume, um dem Besucher die Orientierung und die Unterscheidung zwischen *wichtig* und *ganz wichtig* leicht zu ermöglichen. Und: Jedes Raumbild sollte als eine nonverbale Kommunikation verstanden werden, als verbunden mit einer eindeutigen oder mehrdeutigen Botschaft.

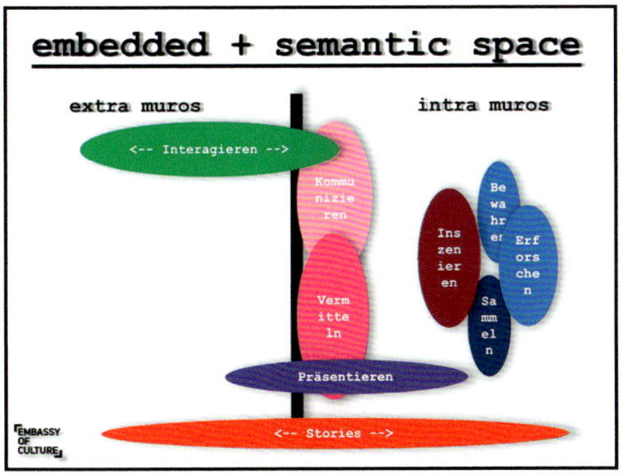

embedded and semantic space (eingebettet und bedeutungsvoll)

Aus diesem hier vorgestellten Repertoire – wenn man so will, eine Erweiterung bzw. Differenzierung des ICOM Code of Ethics for Museums – ließe sich ein jeweils auf die Eigenheiten eines Museums zugeschnittenes authentisches Profil entwickeln. Dabei ist Einzigartigkeit ein wichtiges Merkmal im Kampf um Aufmerksamkeit. Damit sind, gepaart mit dem Aspekt der Wiedererkennbarkeit und einem umfassenden Qualitätsverständnis, zugleich die wesentlichen Elemente eines markenorientierten Managements benannt. Entscheidend ist und bleibt ein ganzheitlicher Blick auf die Institution.

So könnte sich das Museum künftig zu einem semantischen Raum entwickeln:

- bedeutungsvoll – d.h. mit einem geschärften Bewusstsein für das Aufgreifen gesellschaftlich relevanter Themen,
- ruhend in sich selbst – d.h. nicht getrieben, sondern selbstbewusst – im Sinne eines kulturpolitischen Agenda Setting – die Themen setzend,
- eingebettet in die Gesellschaft(en) – und zugleich als deren Resonanzraum dienend,
- bereit zum Dialog mit seinen BesucherInnen – auch außerhalb seiner angestammten Mauern (vgl. outreach[69]),
- auf Augenhöhe – d.h. in der institutionellen Selbstwahrnehmung die Frage der Deutungshoheit stets transparent behandelnd,
- und schließlich proaktiv partizipativ.[70]

Anmerkungen

1 Die Grundkonzeption der Textfassung dieses Vortrags wurde im Oktober 2016 abgeschlossen. Die im Artikel zitierten Links wurden im September 2016 aufgerufen. Im Februar 2018 konnten nur an vereinzelten Stellen aktuelle Verweise nachgetragen werden.

2 ICOM Code of Ethics, S. 29. URL: http://www.icom-deutschland.de/client/media/364/icom_ethische_richtlinien_d_2010.pdf

3 Hermann Auer (Hrsg.): Denkschrift Museen. Zur Lage der Museen in der Bundesrepublik Deutschland und Berlin (West). Boppard 1974, S. 37.

4 Heraklit von Ephesus, um 540–480 v.Chr.

5 Musée imaginaire de la sculpture mondiale. Vgl. URL: http://www.faz.net/aktuell/feuilleton/buecher/rezensionen/sachbuch/walter-grasskamp-ueber-andre-malraux-und-das-imaginaere-museum-12939563.html

6 Ellen Spickernagel und Brigitte Walbe (Hrsgg.): Das Museum. Lernort contra Musentempel. Gießen 1976.

7 Joachim Baur: Ausstellen. Trends und Tendenzen im kulturhistorischen Feld. URL: http://exponauten.de/wp-content/uploads/2017/01/Baur_Denkschrift_131-144.pdf, S. 133

8 Am 7. Oktober 2017 wurde der Neubau und die Neukonzeption des Historischen Museums Frankfurt eröffnet. Mit rund 54 Mio. Euro handelt es sich um ein ausgesprochen ambitioniertes Projekt. Spannend wird es werden, ob die Neukonzeption ähnlich stilbildende Wirkung entfalten wird, wie es – zumindest im museumstheoretischen Diskurs – die Ausstellung der frühen 1970er Jahre tat.

9 URL: http://www.zeit.de/1980/26/aus-dem-land-des-orpheus

10 URL: http://exponauten.de/wp-content/uploads/2017/ 01/Baur_Denkschrift_131-144.pdf, Seite 134. Vgl. auch: Bodo-Michael Baumunk: Der Ausstellungsmacher als Charlatan. Vortrag, Graz 2007, URL: http://bodo-baumunk.net/charlatan.pdf

11 URL: http://www.sehepunkte.de/2012/02/21100.html

12 Wolf-Dieter Könenkamp: Erklärung durch Zusammenhang. Zu Theorie und Praxis der Ausstellung im kulturhistorischen Museum. In: Silke Göttsch und Kai Detlev Sievers (Hrsgg.): Forschungsfeld Museum. FS für Arnold Lühning zum 65. Geburtstag (= Kieler Blätter zur Volkskunde 20). Kiel 1988, S. 137–167.

13 URL: https://de.wikipedia.org/wiki/Mus%C3%A9e_Sentimental mit Ausstellungen in den Jahren 1979, 1981 und 1989. Vgl. auch URL: http://museologien.blogspot. de/2011/12/grazgefluster.html

14 Vgl.: Susanne Gesser u. a. (Hrsgg.): Das partizipative Museum. Zwischen Teilhabe und User Generated Content. Neue Anforderungen an kulturhistorische Ausstellungen. Bielefeld 2012.

15 Gottfried Korff und Martin Roth (Hrsgg.): Das historische Museum. Labor, Schaubühne, Identitätsfabrik. Frankfurt a. M., New York, Paris 1990.

16 Vgl. URL: https://de.wikipedia.org/wiki/Expo_2000

17 Vgl.: Anna Schober: Montierte Geschichten. Programmatisch inszenierte historische Ausstellungen (= Veröffentlichungen des Ludwig-Boltzmann-Institutes für Geschichte der Gesellschaftswissenschaften 24) Wien 1994; Ulrich Schwarz und Philipp Teufel (Hrsgg.): Handbuch Museografie und Ausstellungsgestaltung. Ludwigsburg 2001.

18 Claudia Schulze: Multimedia in Museen. Standpunkte und Perspektiven interaktiver digitaler Systeme im Ausstellungsbereich. Wiesbaden 2001.

19 Auch wenn er schon einige Jahre alt ist, so gibt der Artikel von Schweibenz einen tiefen Einblick in den Stand der damaligen Diskussion. Werner Schweibenz: Das virtuelle Museum. Überlegungen zum Begriff und Wesen des Museums im Internet. URL: http://www.mai-tagung. lvr.de/media/mai_tagung/pdf/2001/schweibenz.pdf

20 URL: http://www.virtualmuseum.ca/virtual-exhibits/exhibit/artpad-a-collection-a-connection/

21 URL: http://www.participatorymuseum.org/

22 Peter Vergor (Hrsg.): The New Museology. London 1989. Vgl. URL: http://framerframed.nl/wp-content/uploads/ 2011/08/SOCIOMUSEOLOGY-TO-UNDERSTAND-NEW-MUSEOLOGY-IN-THE-21ST-CENTURY.pdf – Eine vorzügliche Zusammenstellung relevanter Literatur findet sich hier: URL: https://www.google.de/url?sa=t&rct=j&q= &esrc=s&source=web&cd=1&ved=0ahUKEwjQrLKh5KLPAhWGNxQKHViRCgEQFggiMAA&url=http%3A%22 Fnetwork.icom.museum%2Ffileadmin%2Fuser_upload%2Fminisites%2Fcomcol%2Fother_documents%2FBibliographyParticipation.docx&usg=AFQjCNH4kWGUSwweXx-vC1qVJN1dhqDYWg&sig2=57YXrZO4j9Xrs6TG6 YC6lA&cad=rja Vgl.: Anne van Dam: TO HAVE, TO HOLD, TO SHOW, TO SHARE. A Review of Participatory Curatorial Practices in Theory and Practice in Cultural Institutions Framer Framed. Amsterdam und Leyden 2014. URL: https://www.academia.edu/7121970/A_Review_of_Participatory_Curatorial_Practices_in_Theory _and_Practice_in_Cultural_Institutions?auto=download Richtungweisend war der frühe Artikel von D. Cameron: „The Museum: A Temple or the Forum?" In: Curator. The Museum Journal 14 (1971), S. 11–24.

23 Matthias Henkel: Audience Development – zwischen gesellschaftlicher Teilhabe und Umsatzoptimierung. In: Das Museum für alle: Imperativ oder Illusion? Internationales Bodensee-Symposium am 18.–20. Juni 2015. Ausgerichtet von den Nationalkomitees von ICOM-Schweiz, ICOM-Österreich und ICOM-Deutschland. 2016, S. 34–46.
24 Natalia Grincheva: Cultural Diplomacy 2.0: Challenges and Opportunities in Museum International Practices. In: Museum & Society, 11 (2013), S. 39–49. URL: https:// www2.le.ac.uk/departments/museumstudies/museumsociety/documents/volume s/grincheva.pdf
25 „Mit Big Data werden große Mengen an Daten bezeichnet, [...] die aus Quellen wie intelligenten Agenten, sozialen Medien, Kredit- und Kundenkarten, Smart-Metering-Systemen, Assistenzgeräten, Überwachungskameras sowie Flug- und Fahrzeugen stammen und die mit speziellen Lösungen gespeichert, verarbeitet und ausgewertet werden. Es geht u.a. [...] um (Inter-) Dependenzanalyse, Umfeld- und Trendforschung sowie System- und Produktionssteuerung. Wie im Data Mining ist Wissensentdeckung ein Anliegen. Das weltweite Datenvolumen ist derart angeschwollen, dass bis dato nicht gekannte Möglichkeiten eröffnet werden. Auch die Vernetzung von Datenquellen führt zu neuartigen Nutzungen, zudem zu Risiken für Benutzer und Organisationen." Aus: Gabler Wirtschaftslexikon online, URL: http://wirtschaftslexikon.gabler.de/Definition/big-data.html
26 URL: http://www.faz.net/aktuell/feuilleton/kunst/macron-fordert-endgueltige-restitutionen-des-afrikanisches-erbes-an-afrika-15388474.html
27 URL: https://de.ambafrance.org/Staatsprasident-Macron-in-Ouagadougou-Aufbau-in-Afrika-ist-ein-Projekt-zwischen
28 URL: http://www.lostart.de/Webs/DE/Datenbank/Grundlagen/WashingtonerPrinzipien.html
29 URL: http://www.taskforce-kunstfund.de/chronologie.htm
30 Vgl. Matthias Henkel: SOLILOQUISING ABOUT TRUSTWORTHINESS (Museums as places of Truthfulness). Vortrag gehalten auf der Konferenz von ICOM-MPR in Amsterdam 2017. URL: http://embassy-of-culture.com wp-content/uploads/2017/10/Cultural-Bulletin-of-EoC-4-2017-TRUSTWORTHINESS.pdf
31 Vgl. URL: https://archive.org/stream/pdfy-vNiFct6b-L5ucJEa/Marshall%20McLuhan%20-%20The%20Medium%20is%20The%20Massage#page/n71/mode/2up
32 Vgl. URL: http://www.faz.net/aktuell/feuilleton/kunst/gespraech-mit-frances-morris-von-tate-london-14280114.html?printPagedArticle=true#pageIndex_2
33 Verdienstvoll in diesem Sinne ist die sogenannte MAI-Tagung, die seit über einem Jahrzehnt die Schnittstelle von Museum und Internet bearbeitet. URL: http://www.mai-tagung.lvr.de/de/startseite.html. Vgl. auch URL: http:// www.webmuseen.de/berlin. html
34 Zu den dabei zu beachtenden rechtlichen Aspekten: URL: http://www.iuwis.de/category/freie-tags/digitalisierung-von-museumsbest%C3%A4nden Vgl.: Thomas Dreier u. a. (Hrsgg.): Informationen der öffentlichen Hand. Zugang und Nutzung (= Studien zur Informationsfreiheit 3). Baden-Baden 2016. Zu politischen Initiativen: URL: https://www.landtag.nrw.de/portal/WWW/dokumentenarchiv/Dokument?Id=MMD16/ 10422 – Zu laufenden großen Projekten vgl. Deutsche Digitale Bibliothek und Europeana. Der sachliche Auftritt von http://www.museum-digital.de/ umfasst beispielsweise derzeit lediglich 101.520 Objekte aus 477 Museen und 2070 Sammlungen – d.h. im Durchschnitt 212 Objekte pro beteiligtes Museum.
35 Vgl. Matthias Henkel: Curating the Content in the Digital Space. Oder: Wie man mit Twitter und Facebook einer historischen Person folgen kann. In: Tagungsband der 23. Veranstaltung der internationalen EVA-Serie. Berlin 2016, S. 142–148.
36 URL: https://twitter.com/search?q=%23AskACurator& src=tyah
37 URL: https://www.google.com/culturalinstitute/beta/
38 Beat Wyss: Beim Google Art Project fehlt, was bisher störte. URL: https://www.welt.de/kultur/article12511404/Beim-Google-Art-Project-fehlt-was-bisher-stoerte.html
39 URL: https://www.kunstmatrix.com/de
40 URL: https://virtuelles-migrationsmuseum.org/2014/02/ 19/trailer/
41 URL: https://www.adidas-archive.org/#/ourheroes/Beckenbauer
42 URL: https://museumhack.com/
43 Bring Your Own Device
44 Dieser Artikel gibt einen recht guten Einblick in den Stand der Diskussion zur Medialisierung des Museums: http://www.n24.de/n24/Wissen/Kultur-Gesellschaft/d/6619862/museen-wollen-multimedia-statt-audioguide. html
45 Vgl. dazu den Tagungsbericht: http://culture-to-go.com/2014/05/30/museum-und-internet-neue-tendenzen-auf-der-mai-tagung/

46 Inwiefern die neue Datenschutz-Grundverordnung (EU-DSGVO) oder die Diskussion um Datensicherheit – befeuert durch die Untersuchungen gegen Facebook in Zusammenhang mit der Trump-Wahl – eine neue Kultur des informationsbezogenen Selbstverständnisses erzeugen werden, wird sich erst in der Rückschau bewerten lassen. Wertet man den derzeitigen Börsenkurs von Facebook als Indikator, darf die mediale Aufregung über die Fremdnutzung von Nutzerdaten als kommunikatives Zwischentief bereits ad acta gelegt werden.

47 Entscheidend ist hier eine eindeutige rechtliche Regelung zur sogenannten Störerhaftung. Vgl. URL: http://www.computerbild.de/artikel/cb-News-Internet-EuGH-Urteil-zur-Stoererhaftung-entlastet-WLAN-Anbieter-16328281.html

48 Ein wahrer Pop-Star unter den Kuratoren scheint der Archäologe Irving Finkel zu sein. Vgl. URL: https:// www.youtube.com/watch?v=sbfr-9US31k&list=PL0LQM0SA x603A6p5EJ9DVcESqQReT7QyK

49 Hier mit einem Angebot an die Besucher, unter den über 100.000 Objekten eine eigene digitale Kollektion anzulegen: URL: https://www.youtube.com/watch?v=57 LR4IW9f4I

50 Allein schon die Musikauswahl macht deutlich, dass hier insbesondere junge Zielgruppen angesprochen werden sollen. URL: https://www.youtube.com/watch?v= SXtod_0iDbI

51 Intro-Video zur Vorstellung des Hauses (Länge 1:30 Min.): URL: https://www.youtube.com/watch?v=AOqd CNjq-x0

52 URL: https://www.youtube.com/watch?v=FYdXfQHOE64 (Aufrufe <2.500 am 24.09.2016)

53 Der hier ausgewählte Film dient zur Bewerbung eines besonderen Partizipationsangebotes: der Erstellung eines eigenen Merchandising-Produktes (Rijksstudio Award): https://www.rijksmuseum.nl/en/rijksstudio-award

54 URL: http://www.tanjapraske.de/museumsblogroll/

55 URL: http://museummedia.nl/links/100-best-curator-and-museum-blogs/

56 Hier mit einem Beitrag zu Tischbeins berühmtem Goethe-Bild: http://blog.staedelmuseum.de/goethe-in-der-roemischen-campagna-frankfurts-mona-lisa-hat-zwei-linke-fuesse/

57 Die Diskussion in Bezug auf die Nutzung in Museen ist derzeit noch in Gang und wird sicherlich kontrovers bleiben. Vgl. URL: https://blogs.ucl.ac.uk/museums/2016/ 08/02/why-pokemon-go-is-a-gift-to-museums/ sowie URL: http://openmuseum.de/stop-und-pokemon-go-im-museum/ In jedem Falle ist die Schnittstelle zwischen Learning und Gaming auch für den Bereich der kulturellen Bildung relevant.

58 URL: https://de.wikipedia.org/wiki/Newsdesk

59 Matthias Henkel: Intangible Heritage 2.0. How to collect, curate and present the digital landscape as the new public space. Vortrag gehalten auf der Generalkonferenz von ICOM 2016 in Mailand. URL: https://www.researchgate.net/publication/305904613_Intangible_Heritage_20_ How_to_collect_curate_and_present_the_digital_landscape_as_the_new_public_spacePaper_presented_at_the_Joint_Session_ICFA_Museums_and_Collections_ of_Fine_Arts_and_COMCOL_Collecti

60 http://www.ovrdrv.com/the-3-truths-of-content-strategy/

61 Jürgen Habermas: Die Neue Unübersichtlichkeit. Frankfurt 1985.

62 Vgl. URL: http://upload-magazin.de/blog/9469-influencer-marketing-i-was-sind-influencer-und-wie-findet-man-sie/ sowie URL: http://upload-magazin.de/blog/9472-influencer-marketing-ii-zielsetzungen-und-korrekte-ansprache/ http://www.jeffbullas.com/2014/08/18/is-it-time-to-forget-free-social-media-marketing/

63 Ray Oldenburg: The Great Good Place: Cafes, Coffee Shops, Community Centers, Beauty Parlors, General Stores, Bars, Hangouts, and How They Get You Through the Day. New York 1989.

64 Vgl. URL: http://www.interculture-journal.com/index. php/icj/article/download/209/307

65 In diesem Zusammenhang sei auf die aktuelle Publikation von Nina Simon hingewiesen: Nina Simon: The art of relevance. Santa Cruz 2016.

66 In diesen Film werden historische niederländische Ölgemälde überaus zeitgenössisch präsentiert: https://www.youtube.com/watch?v=d3Y-wTIkErM (Aufrufe >13.000 am 24.09.2016)

67 Vgl. Matthias Henkel: Intangible Heritage in the Digital Era. S. 93–98. URL: https://issuu.com/museumid/docs/ museumid_issue20

68 Vgl. URL: https://www.usability.gov/what-and-why/visual-design.html

69 Vgl. URL: https://www.kubi-online.de/artikel/museen-outreach

70 Vgl.: Anja Piontek: Partizipative Ansätze in Museen und deren Bildungsarbeit (2016). URL: https://www.kubi-online.de/artikel/partizipative-ansaetze-museen-deren-bildungsarbeit

DIE AUTOREN

Dr. Anne-Lise Desmas is senior curator and department head of sculpture and decorative arts at the J. Paul Getty Museum in Los Angeles. She specializes in European sculpture before 1900, with emphasis on French and Italian sculpture of the seventeenth and eighteenth centuries.

Dr. Matthias Henkel ist Mitglied im Leitungsteam des Zentrums für Audience Development/IKM an der Freien Universität Berlin und Inhaber der Agentur EMBASSY OF CULTURE.

Dr. Katarina Horst studierte klassische Archäologie und Kunstgeschichte und durchlief ab 1997 ihre Museumslaufbahn im Badischen Landesmuseum Karlsruhe. Seit 2012 ist sie Leiterin der Abteilung Wissenschaft und Sammlungen im Badischen Landesmuseum Karlsruhe. Schwerpunkte in ihrer Museumsarbeit sind der Kulturgutschutz, der interkulturelle Dialog und die inhaltliche Neuausrichtung des Museums.

Dr. Uta Piereth ist Museumsreferentin der Bayerischen Schlösserverwaltung, zuständig für die Cadolzburg sowie für Bildung und Vermittlung.

BILDNACHWEIS

ANNE-LISE DESMAS

Abb. 1–20 | Fotos: Anne-Lise Desmas

KATARINA HORST

Abb. 1, 8, 9, 11 | Foto: Katarina Horst
Abb. 2 | Foto: Ch. Kiefer. Aus: Hess 2014, S. 46, Abb. 1.
Abb. 3 | Foto: H. Hübsch. Aus: Hess 2014, S. 117, Abb. 3.
Abb. 4 | Aus: Maaß 1988, S. 84, Abb. 59.
Abb. 5 | Aus: Grimm 1993, S. 150, Abb. 113.
Abb. 6 | Aus: Grimm 1993, S. 188, Abb. 146.
Abb. 7 | Foto: Thomas Goldschmidt, Badisches Landesmuseum
Abb. 10 | Foto: Thomas Goldschmidt, Badisches Landesmuseum

UTA PIERETH

Abb. 1 | Foto: Nürnberg Luftbild/Hajo Dietz
Abb. 2–16 | Foto: Bayerische Verwaltung der staatlichen Schlösser, Gärten und Seen (BSV)

MATTHIAS HENKEL

Grafiken: Matthias Henkel

BIBLIOGRAPHIE

Aumann, Philipp / Frank Duerr: Ausstellungen machen (= UTB 3892). Paderborn [2]2014.

Alder, Barbara / Barbara den Brok: Die perfekte Ausstellung. Ein Praxisleitfaden zum Projektmanagement von Ausstellungen (= Praxis Guide n.n.). Bielefeld 2012.

Assmann, Aleida: Konstruktion von Geschichte in Museen. In: Aus Politik und Zeitgeschichte 49 (2007), S. 6–13, URL: http://www.bpb.de/apuz/30058/museen-und-gesellschaft (Stand: 28.10.2018).

Assmann, Aleida: Erinnerungsräume. Formen und Wandlungen des kulturellen Gedächtnisses (= C.-H.-Beck-Kullturwissenschaft n.n.). München [5]2010.

Barchet, Michael / Donata Koch-Haag / Karl Sierek (Hgg.): Ausstellen. Der Raum der Oberfläche. Weimar 2003.

Baur, Joachim (Hg.): Museumsanalyse. Methoden und Konturen eines neuen Forschungsfeldes (= Schriften zum Kultur- und Museumsmanagement n.n.). Bielefeld [2]2013.

Beier-de Haan / Marie-Paule Jungblut (Hgg.): Das Ausstellen und das Immaterielle (= Beiträge der 1. Museologischen Studientage Neumünster. Luxemburg 2006). München 2007.

Berg, Karen van den / Hans Ulrich Gumbrecht (Hgg.): Politik des Zeigens. München u.a. 2010.

Bosse, Dagmar / Michael Glasmeier / Agnes Prus (Hgg.): Der Ausstellungskatalog. Beiträge zur Geschichte und Theorie. Köln 2004.

Bröckers, Hannah: Der Museumsbesuch als Event. Museen in der Erlebnisgesellschaft (= Mitteilungen und Berichte aus dem Institut für Museumsforschung 37). Berlin 2007.

Brückle, Wolfgang / Pierre Alain Mariaux / Daniela Mondini (Hgg.): Musealisierung mittelalterlicher Kunst. Anlässe, Ansätze, Ansprüche. Berlin / München 2015.

Brüderlin, Markus: Die Aura des White Cube. Der sakrale Raum und seine Spuren im modernen Ausstellungsraum. In: Zeitschrift für Kunstgeschichte 76 (2013), S. 91–106.

Clifford, James: Museums as Contact Zones. In: ders. (Hg.): Routes. Travel and Translation in the Late Twentieth Century. Cambridge (MA) / London 1997, S. 188–219.

Coelsch-Foisner, Sabine / Douglas Brown (Hgg.): The Museal Turn (= Wissenschaft und Kunst 22). Heidelberg 2012.

Collenberg-Plotnikov, Bernadette (Hg.): Musealisierung und Reflexion. Gedächtnis, Erinnerung, Geschichte (= Kunst als Kulturgut 3). München 2011.

Cramer, Iris: Kunstvermittlung in Ausstellungskatalogen. Eine typologische Rekonstruktion (= Europäische Hochschulschriften 28). Frankfurt a. M. u.a. 1998.

Davis, Ann / Kerstin Smeds (Hgg.): Visiting the Visitor. An Enquiry Into the Visitor Business in Museums (= Edition Museum 18). Bielefeld 2016.

Dernie, David: Ausstellungsgestaltung. Konzepte und Techniken. Ludwigsburg 2006.

Eigenheer, Marianne (Hg.): Curating Critique (= ICE-Reader 1). Frankfurt a. M. 2007.

Gesser, Susanne / Martin Handschin / Angela Jannelli / Sibylle Lichtensteiger (Hgg.): Das partizipative Museum. Zwischen Teilhabe und User Generated Content. Neue Anforderungen an kulturhistorische Ausstellungen (= Schriften zum Kultur- und Museumsmanagement n.n.). Bielefeld 2012.

Gfrereis, Heike / Thomas Thiemeyer / Bernhard Tschofen (Hgg.): Museen verstehen. Begriffe der Theorie und Praxis (= Marbacher Schriften. Neue Folge 11). Göttingen / Wallstein 2015.

Graf, Bernhard / Volker Rodekamp (Hgg.): Museen zwischen Qualität und Relevanz. Denkschrift zur

Lage der Museen (= Berliner Schriftenreihe zur Museumsforschung 30). Berlin 2012.
Grasskamp, Walter: Das Kunstmuseum. Eine erfolgreiche Fehlkonstruktion (= C.H. Beck Paperback 6228). München 2016.
Grießer, Martina / Christine Haupt-Stummer (Hgg.): Handbuch Ausstellungstheorie und -praxis (= UTB 3759). Wien u.a. 2013.
Grincheva, Natalia: Cultural Diplomacy 2.0. Challenges and Opportunities in Museum International Practices. In: Museum & Society 11 (2013), S. 39–49.
Habsburg-Lothringen, Bettina: Dauerausstellungen. Schlaglichter auf ein Format (= Edition Museumsakademie Joanneum 3). Bielefeld 2012.
Hanak-Lettner, Werner: Die Ausstellung als Drama. Wie das Museum aus dem Theater entstand. Bielefeld 2011.
Hantelmann, Dorothea, von (Hg.): Die Ausstellung. Politik eines Rituals. Zürich u.a. 2010.
Hartung, Olaf (Hg.): Museum und Geschichtskultur. Ästhetik – Politik – Wissenschaft (= Sonderveröffentlichungen der Gesellschaft für Kieler Stadtgeschichte 52). Gütersloh 2006.
Hemken, Kai-Uwe (Hg.): Kritische Szenografie. Die Kunstausstellung im 21. Jahrhundert (= Image 64). Bielefeld 2015.
Heesen, Anke te / Petra Lutz (Hgg.): Dingwelten. Das Museum als Erkenntnisort (= Schriften des Deutschen Hygiene-Museums Dresden 4). Köln u.a. 2005.
Heesen, Anke te: Theorien des Museums zur Einführung (= Zur Einführung 398). Hamburg ^{3}2015.
Hoins, Katharina / Felicitas von Mallinckrodt (Hgg.): Macht, Wissen, Teilhabe. Sammlungsinstitutionen im 21. Jahrhundert (= Dresdner Schriften zu Kultur und Wissen 1). Bielefeld 2015.
John, Hartmut / Anja Dauschek (Hgg.): Museen neu denken. Perspektiven der Kulturvermittlung und Zielgruppenarbeit (= Publikationen der Abteilung Museumsberatung. Landschaftsverband Rheinland 26). Bielefeld 2008.
Kaiser, Brigitte: Inszenierung und Erlebnis in kulturhistorischen Ausstellungen. Museale Kommunikation in kunstpädagogischer Perspektive (= Schriften zum Kultur- und Museumsmanagement n.n.). Bielefeld 2006.
Kirchhoff, Heike / Martin Schmidt (Hgg.): Das magische Dreieck. Die Museumsausstellung als Zusammenspiel von Kuratoren, Museumspädagogen und Gestaltern. Kultur- und Museumsmanagement (= Schriften des Bundesverbands freiberuflicher Kulturwissenschaftler 1). Bielefeld 2007.
Klein, Alexander: Expositum. Zum Verhältnis von Ausstellung und Wirklichkeit. Bielefeld 2004.
Klonk, Charlotte: Spaces of Experience. Art Gallery Interiors from 1800 to 2000. New Haven u.a. 2009.
Klonk, Charlotte: Sichtbar machen und sichtbar werden im Kunstmuseum. In: Gottfried Boehm / Sebastian Egenhofer / Christian Spies (Hgg.): Zeigen. Die Rhetorik des Sichtbaren (= Eikones n.n.). München 2010, S. 291–312.
Knell, Simon J. / Peter Aronsson / Arne Bugge Amundsen (Hgg.): National Museums. New Studies from Around the World. London u.a. 2011.
Knell, Simon J.: National Galleries. The Art of Making Nations. London / New York 2016.
Könenkamp, Wolf-Dieter: Erklärung durch Zusammenhang. Zu Theorie und Praxis der Ausstellung im kulturhistorischen Museum. In: Silke Göttsch-Elten / Kai Detlev Sievers (Hgg.): Forschungsfeld Museum. FS für Arnold Lühning zum 65. Geburtstag (= Kieler Blätter zur Volkskunde 20). Kiel / Mühlau 1988, S. 137–167.
Korff, Gottfried / Martin Roth (Hgg.): Das historische Museum. Labor, Schaubühne, Identitätsfabrik. Frankfurt a.M. / New York / Paris 1990.
Korff, Gottfried / Martina Eberspächer / Bodo-Michael Baumunk (Hgg.): Museumsdinge. Deponieren – exponieren. Köln u.a. ^{2}2007.
Macdonald, Sharon: New Constellations of Difference in Europe's 21st-Century Museumscape. In: Museum Anthropology 39.1 (2016), S. 4–19.
Mai, Ekkehard: Expositionen. Geschichte und Kritik des Ausstellungswesens. München 1986.
Mai, Ekkehard (Hg.): Die Zukunft der Alten Meister. Perspektiven und Konzepte für das Kunstmuseum von heute. Köln / Weimar / Wien 2001.
Meyer, Andrea / Bénédicte Savoy (Hgg.): The Museum Is Open. Towards a Transnational History of Museums 1750–1940 (= Contact Zones 1). Berlin / Boston 2014.
Mihatsch, Karin: Der Ausstellungskatalog 2.0. Vom Printmedium zur Online-Repräsentation von Kunstwerken. Über Repräsentationsformen von Kunstwerken und deren Kontext im Web 2.0 (= Edition Museum 12). Bielefeld 2015.

Murawska-Muthesius, Katarzyna / Piotr Piotrowski (Hgg.): From Museum Critique to the Critical Museum. Farnham / Burlington / Ashgate 2015.

Muttenthaler, Roswitha / Regina Wonisch: Gesten des Zeigens. Zur Repräsentation von Gender und Race in Ausstellungen (= Schriften zum Kultur- und Museumsmanagement n.n.). Bielefeld 2006.

Padberg, Martina / Martin Schmidt (Hgg.): Die Magie der Geschichte. Geschichtskultur und Museum (= Schriften des Bundesverbands freiberuflicher Kulturwissenschaftler 3). Bielefeld 2010.

Piontek, Anja: Museum und Partizipation. Theorie und Praxis kooperativer Ausstellungsprojekte und Beteiligungsangebote (= Edition Museum 26). Bielefeld 2017.

Pöhlmann, Wolfger: Handbuch zur Ausstellungspraxis von A bis Z (= Berliner Schriften zur Museumsforschung 5). Berlin 2007.

Pomian, Krzysztof: Der Ursprung des Museums. Vom Sammeln (= Kleine kulturwissenschaftliche Bibliothek 9). Berlin 1988.

Rettore Waser, Claudia (Hg.): Das Museum für alle – Imperativ oder Illusion? Internationales Bodensee-Symposium. 18.–20. Juni 2015. Zürich 2016, URL: https://www.museums.ch/assets/files/dossiers_d/Publikationen/Bodenseesymposium2015_web.pdf (Stand: 28.10.2018).

Reussner, Eva Maria: Publikumsforschung für Museen. Internationale Erfolgsbeispiele. Die Öffnung von Museen für ihr Publikum (= Schriften zum Kultur- und Museumsmanagament n.n.). Bielefeld 2010.

Saalmann, Timo: Die Kunstpolitik der Berliner Museen. 1919 – 1959 (= Schriften zur modernen Kunsthistoriographie 6). Berlin 2014.

Schärer, Martin R.: Die Ausstellung. Theorie und Exempel. München 2003.

Schober, Anna: Montierte Geschichten. Programmatisch inszenierte historische Ausstellungen (= Veröffentlichungen des Ludwig-Boltzmann-Institutes für Geschichte der Gesellschaftswissenschaften 24). Wien 1994.

Scholze, Jana: Medium Ausstellung. Lektüren musealer Gestaltung in Oxford, Leipzig, Amsterdam und Berlin (= Schriften zum Kultur- und Museumsmanagement n.n.). Bielefeld 2004.

Schulze, Claudia: Multimedia in Museen. Standpunkte und Perspektiven interaktiver digitaler Systeme im Ausstellungsbereich (= DUV Sozialwissenschaft n.n.). Wiesbaden 2001.

Schwan, Stephan / Helmuth Trischler / Manfred Prenzel (Hgg.): Lernen im Museum. Die Rolle von Medien. Kunst als Kommunikationsinstrument in Unternehmen (= Mitteilungen und Berichte aus dem Institut für Museumskunde 38). Berlin 2006.

Schwarz, Ulrich / Philipp Teufel (Hgg.): Handbuch Museografie und Ausstellungsgestaltung. Ludwigsburg 2001.

Spickernagel, Ellen / Brigitte Walbe (Hgg.): Das Museum. Lernort contra Musentempel (= Kritische Berichte. Sonderbd.). Gießen ²1976.

Strunck, Christina / Elisabeth Kieven (Hgg.): Europäische Galeriebauten. Galleries in a Comparative European Perspective (= Römische Studien der Bibliotheca Hertziana 29). München 2010.

Thiemeyer, Thomas: Werk, Exemplar, Zeuge. Die multiplen Authentizitäten der Museumsdinge. In: Martin Sabrow / Achim Saupe (Hgg.): Historische Authentizität. Göttingen 2016, S. 80–90.

Vergo, Peter (Hg.): The New Museology. London 1989.

Vieregg, Hildegard: Museumswissenschaften. Eine Einführung (= UTB 2823). Paderborn 2006.

Walz, Markus (Hg.): Handbuch Museum. Geschichte, Aufgaben, Perspektiven. Stuttgart 2016.

Wegner, Nora: Publikumsmagnet Sonderausstellung – Stiefkind Dauerausstellung? Erfolgsfaktoren einer zielgruppenorientierten Museumsarbeit (= Schriften zum Kultur- und Museumsmanagement n.n.). Bielefeld 2015.